SO-AEZ-084

My Pulse,
His Will
*Tragedy to Triumph that
Echoed her Faith*

Jessica Lyngaas

BALBOA.
PRESS

A DIVISION OF HAY HOUSE

Copyright © 2016 Jessica Lyngaas.

All rights reserved. No part of this book may be used or reproduced by any means, graphic, electronic, or mechanical, including photocopying, recording, taping or by any information storage retrieval system without the written permission of the author except in the case of brief quotations embodied in critical articles and reviews.

Unless otherwise indicated all Scripture quotation are from The Holy Bible English Standard Version (ESV). Copyright 2001 by Crossway.

All scriptures in the Everyday Life Bible is taken from the Amplified Bible (AMP). Copyright 1954, 1958, 1962, 1964, 1965, 1987 by the Lockman Foundation.

Balboa Press books may be ordered through booksellers or by contacting:

Balboa Press
A Division of Hay House
1663 Liberty Drive
Bloomington, IN 47403
www.balboapress.com
1 (877) 407-4847

Because of the dynamic nature of the Internet, any web addresses or links contained in this book may have changed since publication and may no longer be valid. The views expressed in this work are solely those of the author and do not necessarily reflect the views of the publisher, and the publisher hereby disclaims any responsibility for them.

The author of this book does not dispense medical advice or prescribe the use of any technique as a form of treatment for physical, emotional, or medical problems without the advice of a physician, either directly or indirectly. The intent of the author is only to offer information of a general nature to help you in your quest for emotional and spiritual well-being. In the event you use any of the information in this book for yourself, which is your constitutional right, the author and the publisher assume no responsibility for your actions.

Any people depicted in stock imagery provided by Thinkstock are models, and such images are being used for illustrative purposes only.
Certain stock imagery © Thinkstock.

Print information available on the last page.

ISBN: 978-1-5043-6693-9 (sc)
ISBN: 978-1-5043-6695-3 (hc)
ISBN: 978-1-5043-6694-6 (e)

Library of Congress Control Number: 2016916010

Balboa Press rev. date: 10/04/2016

CONTENTS

FOREWORD

Jessica comes from a plains state growing up in a traditional Catholic, farm family where faith, family, and hard work are those core values that are instilled at a young age an have been encouraged from generation of the past. Jessica is strong rooted in all these values and as you read this book finding how those values have carried her through the realities in life and all its challenges.

At one time or another we all have had some tragedy or turmoil and it appears that it seems to compound itself all at once and we all feel "Why us? What is next? Etc..." We for the most part recover from this hurdle and we then resume our normal routines. As for some how we cope with these events they can drive our emotions, daily living, self esteem, and health. Depending on the events sometimes the preconceived notion of a persons response to trauma one may see or expect the person affected to become addicted to chemicals, become emotionally or behaviorally changed and/or self worth of one's self to crash.

As you read you will see how Jessica and her family have maintained, adapted, and continues to move forward daily. From a debilitating car accident, multiple health issues, maintaining a household, financially making ends meet, raising children with support from her life partner, stability, adaptations and core values and strong faith have helped. When a tragedy takes that away in a heartbeat one can ask what is next and want to give up. Jessica is now forced to make life and death decisions and whats in store from these choices is so amazing. Becoming a widow, becoming the soul bread winner, raising a family and trying to maintain a home setting as close as possible prior to theses events is definitely a task.

As Life challenges can control us, observe how she utilizes her abilities and accepts the path God places in front of her. A favorite quote that both of us live by is "When God is placed first, whatever comes second will always be right." As each life event continues to occur for Jessica she keeps her Faith and continues on in an upward, forward, and positive direction, both physically and spiritually.

Coming from an area of small towns you get to know many people. As an outsider looking in, sharing in commonalities with Jessica, Lance, and their kids as well as Jessica's family seeing life as it unveils of the hurdles overcome is quite impressive. As life events have happened and have brought Jessica and I together has been truly a path planned by God before us. As God places paths, people in and out of our lives it is our choosing to which path we take. Through the why's of those things we control by choices and the how we deal and accept the why's of the things we do not control.

It is constantly amazing how Jessica's strong faith and will shines as Life has given her and her family many trials. Some stereotype and expect the 'wounded bird' presentation of a single parent and grieving wife, hence the writing of this book to tell a story and guide others as the tools she has applied as the question is always posed to her "How do you do it Jessica?" Like a mother bear she is strong, guides her 'cubs', protects what is important, and has strong, consistent Faith that leads her to her destination. Please read this journey of her's with an open mind and heart.

Christopher Todd Clark

CHAPTER 1

Smile, Love, Laugh

It all began the summer of 1993. Every summer around the different rural communities in our area, street dances would take place for a night of entertainment. I was with my older sister and a very good friend. It was June 4. We went to Herman, MN as Johnny Holmes was playing at the Herman Street Dance. He always and still does put on an awesome show.

That evening my sister, friend, and I ended up running into Lance Lyngaas and his brother. It was fun catching up with class mates and their siblings other then events of school functions. This particular day had so much significance for both Lance and his brother. It marked the one year anniversary of their dad's death. His name was Larry Lyngaas. Larry was an amazing man and an awesome father.

Little did I know then what milestone this particular night would mean for myself in the future. The summer flew by as they always seem to. A spark had been started and Lance and I continued to see each other. This summer happened to be the summer before my junior year in high school. Though I was quite busy with work and so was Lance, we always managed to find the time to go out once a week.

One evening the two of us were out for supper and out of the blue he says "You know I always told my dad I'm going to marry that

Putnam girl." Speechless to say the least I said "you did?' He replied with "Yeah, I did and I wasn't talking about your older sister."

My thoughts at the moment: Let's back up the train a minute. I haven't even started my junior year in high school!! I wasn't thinking marriage and for that matter didn't think we were that serious in our relationship!!

Time progressed and Lance and I became more fond of each other. Little did I know what God had in store for us. We were very limited with our time that we shared with one another due to Lance was a farmer/trucker and gone most of the time. I too was a student, worked every weekend, and the fact that I grew up having strict parents who only allowed us to go out one night a week made this dating issue more challenging then I expected.

Working hard was the only option we really had growing up. My older sister and I worked at an Egg Ranch and we also helped out on our family farm. I also had three younger siblings which were a huge part of my world. Growing up in a family of five children brought many experience of realizing how 'time' is precious and that it takes everyone's cooperation to make everything flow.

The end of August came and my sister went off to college in Brookings, SD and oh how the changes began! My two younger sisters are five and 10 years younger than I and my bother is 12 years younger then me. It definitely has its pros and cons (age difference). For the most part I always felt more like a caregiver versus a fun-playing-sibling. Nevertheless, my bringing up as a teenager taught me many life skills. My goal always was to live simply, love, and help others unconditionally.

In March 1994 Lance proposed to me and on June 17, 1995 we married. Our wedding took place at St Galls Catholic Church in

Tintah, MN. The Late Father Al Stangel united us in marriage and Father Andy Marthaler co-celebrated with Father Al.

Oh, it was a very hot day! 103 degrees outside and 101 degrees inside the church. The wedding was huge and the pews were packed with 350+ people. The ceremony was about an hour and 20 minutes long and I loved every minute of it. It truly did not feel that long.

Father Al gave the most awesome message in his sermon. It was real simple and clearly defines how a marriage can work. He said "marriage is like a tripod; you have God on one leg, husband on the other, and the wife on the third leg. At any point if one of these three legs are absent, the tripod will fall."

Never having difficulty understanding this concept Lance and I grew our marriage stronger and stronger with this solid foundation underneath us. Time progressed and on May 11, 1996 we were blessed with our first son, Levi Lance Lyngaas. The miracle of a child is unbelievable. It is the most rewarding gift you can be given.

This new package that we created is beyond words. I remember thinking "I'm a mom and Lance is a dad! This is and has already been an adventure!" Never slowing down for much, Levi was the 'new' with all of our doings.

This first year zipped by and on October 22, 1997 our second son arrived, Lucas Larry Lyngaas. Lucas was my most content baby. He loved to snuggle. The remarkable beauty, love, and joy we were continually reminded of through these two boys defined how wonderful our life really was.

A couple weeks after Lucas was born we had devastation land in our world. On November 13, we had Lucas baptized and then the next day Lance left for work around 8AM. He worked for a local farmer and enjoyed going to work their always. Farming was his energy, passion, and Joy!!

The morning continued on and I had just got the boys down for a nap. Around 10AM the door opens to our house and in walked Lance. I said "Hey, done for the day?" He looked at me, he was pale in color... I then said "what's wrong Lance? You look sick. Are you OK?" Struggling with words he said "No, I'm not sick. I do not have a job anymore!" I asked "what happened?" Bewildered to say the least, this being both of us, he said "evidently some of my co-workers have differences with me and no longer want to work with me. My co-workers told the Boss that If they didn't get rid of me, the two of them would quit. So they figured it would be better to get rid of one then to lose two employees." In complete shock, I didn't know what to say except "I'm sorry Honey. Trust that there must be something better out there for you."

To this day I still get choked up thinking about it. The pain, suffering, and frustration I saw in Lance that day and how he felt like a failure makes me sick!! People can be so destructive and selfish and when they can act so cowardly and not address issues in a civil manner is very heartbreaking!

The truth, Lance was a Heck of a worker and could do circles around most with everything he did. Jealousy, insecurity, or whatever the reason was, we will never know. But honestly, I wouldn't wish these circumstances on anyone. It was tough and it didn't just affect Lance it affected his bride and two young babies.

Worry and fear constantly trying to set in. I never worried about where our next dollar was coming from because Lance knew how to work and I knew how to be frugal. We also had an awesome God!! I believed then all would work out and I believe this now.

Much anger and frustration began to build up for me. When you live in a small town, situations like this that can occur create a huge wall of hate! I could not allow this turmoil that began in our community slow me down and make me out to be someone I am not. Difficult to say the least. Life continued on. Hardened hearts? Absolutely, and I put my trust in God and sought faith for my future.

Another year came and went and November 17, 1998 are beautiful baby girl entered our world. Morgan Mary Lyngaas. Life was so fun. I had three babies, awesome husband, and wonderful father to my kidlits! I could not have asked for anything more. Family time was huge and everything we did we did it the five of us together or it wasn't going to take place. The kids grew up going to Mass 2-3 times a week, riding on four wheelers and snowmobiles, riding in tractors, quietly riding along on crop tours, visiting and helping the elderly, and constantly surrounded with love and joy! Life was good! We had our ups and down as most families experience, and we also had our solid foundation of our Lord!

It now was June 2000, the children were 2, 3, and 4, years old and I had gone back to college to become a nurse. Lance was an over-the-road truck driver and life was crazy!! Its all a blur as a matter of fact. I worked a couple years as an LPN and then in January of 2003 I was accepted into the RN program. The summer session began in June. Working as a student, mother, wife, and nurse, consumed my every hour of the day.

In August we had a fellow parishioner and good friend of the family who had passed away due to an airplane accident. His name was Richard Johnson, a very kind, helpful, and caring person. He had crashed his plane near his home. It was a very sad and unforgettable day. The Sunday prior to his accident I remember him and his wife taking off in his ultra-light aircraft after Mass.

He was wearing a plaid shirt and great smile. He and his wife waved at everyone and flew off to the east. Little did we all know than that this Sunday was the last time we would see him waving to anyone.

The summer continued on and time passed quickly as it seems to after one leaves us here on earth. Keeping busy also helped me through the loss and refocused my thoughts. My summer semester ended August 9, and the fall session was starting back up on August 15. With only having a couple days off of school, picking up work was much needed.

It was Monday morning August 13, 2003. I was a home health nurse working between two different agencies and also at a local hospital. My sitter arrive to my house to watch our kids at 7AM. Lance had already left for that day and he was working at a local Ag aviation company and there was many acres for the plane to spray. Levi was the only one up that morning before I left and I told him I would see him at 3 in the afternoon.

I had just left my second clients home and it was a couple minutes after 12 noon and down the road two miles, my world stopped. Literally stopped! I was greeted by a very large truck! An orange County truck to be exact!

It was August so the cornfields were tall and beautiful, therefore making 'walls' that blocked your view. I knew there was an intersection coming up so I had slowed down quite a bit as you never know what may be at an intersection. This truck was southbound and I was eastbound. I had the right away. He had a yield sign and corn fields on either side of him. Needless to say T-boned is the term they used.

This was that day I became a critical patient. I was awake for the entire duration of this horrific event, and I never was alone. The gentleman that hit me was talking to me, though I couldn't see him. He assured me he had called 911 and help was on its way.

All of a sudden I looked to my right and there was somebody in the vehicle sitting with me. It was so hot and dusty and I just wanted to bust out of the car. The good Lord knew that was my intention and so he sent me an angel to save my life. His name is Richard Johnson. Richard said to me "Don't move! Your neck is broken! I can see the ambulance approaching."

I felt a sense of calmness overwhelm me and at that point I did not move. I knew the severity of a broken neck and what the dire consequences of any movement. When the ambulance arrived, Richard told the First respondents, "Place a c-collar on her immediately! Her neck is broken!" He then assured me everything was going to be alright, and then he was gone, still wearing his plaid shirt.

Fortunately, God was still with me as He had sent the most wonderful, well-trained first responders/Fire-fighters/EMT's who worked diligently to get me out of my car. They cut the roof from my vehicle and carefully extracted me. As I stated previously, I was conscious during the entire incident and recall that the team was actually accompanied by a doctor. After I was taken to a local hospital they discovered that I had a C2 fracture, a left lung pneumothorax caused by 4 fractured ribs, lacerated spleen, and other minor injuries.

Immediately following the CT scan it was determined I would need specialized treatment so I was taken to Meritcare hospital in Fargo. (Now it is called Sanford Hospital) I kept requesting to be knocked out as my pain was horrible. I finally got my wish and I woke up two days later to find myself strapped down with a crown on my head.

This crown, or halo, included stabilizers drilled into the skull to stabilize the head/neck. I was in no shape to have surgery therefore this was my only option to maintain stability of the cervical spine's structure.

My injury was similar to the injury Christopher Reeves, also known for his Superman caricature. He also had a C2 fracture and was on a ventilator and a quadriplegic for the remaining years after his accident.

It is a complete miracle that I am able to walk and breathe on my own. There is no doubt in my mind that we have the most awesome God who is always with us. He gave me a second shot at life and I was able to continue to raise my three young kids. He is so wonderful. He never leaves us!!! Smile, Laugh, Love... Yes I can!!!

Smile, laugh, love: these three words seem so simple, and yet can be very hard at times. When you look at someone and watch their expression you can learn so much.

Do you ever find yourself looking at someone and wondering why that person is smiling at you? "Do I have something on my face or did I spill something on my shirt?" Immediately, our instinct start screaming 'insecurity' we all have done this before and do this, and nine times out of 10 we have no 'flaws', but we do/did have a smile.... A Look that expresses Love, compassion, and the opportunity to 'stop' and 'share' that very moment of time with someone.

A smile speaks volumes, and it sets precedence. For many, not only is it beautiful, it can be very contagious. Once you smile laughing becomes even easier. As I continue writing down my trials and tribulations during this journey here on earth better be prepared for a 100% faith focused process. Before you get the wrong impression of who I am and what I stand for let me assure you I am only human and I am a child of God just like you.

My hope in writing this book is to provide a guide on how to stay confident and solid, and how all can continue to love and, no matter the circumstances, to live with a heart full of dreams, love born from the depths of the soul that embraces every laughter-filled moment.

"And he said to him, "You shall Love the Lord our God with all your heart and with all your soul and with all your mind. This is the great and first commandment. And a second is like it.: You shall love your neighbor as yourself. On these two commandments depend all the Law and the prophets." (Mathew 22: 37-40)

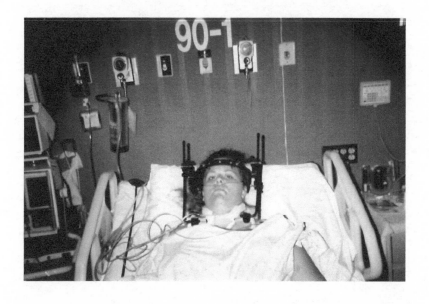

_____

_____

_____

_____

_____

_____

_____

_____

_____

_____

_____

_____

_____

_____

_____

_____

_____

_____

_____

_____

_____

_____

_____

_____

_____

_____

_____

_____

_____

_____

_____

CHAPTER 2

Finding and Maintaining Strength

Eight years past and expanded our experience as parents, siblings, husband, and wife. Watching the kids grow, mature, and begin working for employers themselves, quickly reminded us of how fast time really does go.

This beautiful Sunday began our week, once again together, full of joy, and the usual farm-family productivity. Sharing many smiles, lots of laughs, and continuous love described what occurred on a regular basis in our home.

Mass began Sunday mornings at 8:30 at St Galls Catholic Church in Tintah, MN. On That Morning we were hurrying and scurrying as we rushed down to attend church. Following our church service all of us then assisted our daughter, Morgan, with a special Girl Scout project: landscaping and planting of flowers at the monument which stood on the grounds of the former schoolhouse in town.

The Strength, both physically and mentally that we all incurred as we took direction from Morgan to complete this project is very memorable. Seeing her joy, relief, determination, and all the pride that poured out of her and she had her Dad right at her side helping her accomplish this goal.

Our boys, Levi and Lucas, left for home and Morgan, Lance, and I went to my parents' farm and we had breakfast with my folks. We left Morgan with my Mom to attend a graduation in that afternoon. Lance and I headed for home, but much to my surprise Lance suggested we stop at my grandparents' home in Tintah before we went home. Delighted indeed, we stopped and had a great visit and many laughs.

My grandfather James L Putnam, was a very avid gardener and raised many fruits and vegetables. This being strawberry season, Grandma asked if she could interest us in some fresh strawberry shortcake. It would have been foolish to say no. Grandma Betty dished up our 'treat' in her beautiful glass dessert bowls.

Grandma couldn't get around easily and she walked with assistance of a wheeled walker (the kind with a seat on it, too). I offered to carry the dessert, but to my surprise she said, "It's not every day I get to serve the king, so no, I'm bringing it to Lance." We all giggled, knowing that Grandma's mantra was' where there is a will there is a way.'

Concluding our visit we headed home to our farm. As we were driving home Lance said to me "I feel like I have a 'charlie horse' in my neck.". I thought to myself with much concern that is probably not good, a cramp in the neck? I briefly assessed him, and once we were home, I took his vital signs and they were good. Lance had headaches almost every day and frequently experienced neck pain due to a degenerative disc disease; *to the point that his vertebrae in his cervical spine were 'starred'.* Lance was a bull of a man and his six foot, 230 pound frame was honed by years of heavy lifting on the farm. He was as strong, in both mind and body. As we walked into the house Lance was greeted by the boys. "Dad, can we go for a four-wheeler ride?" "I'm going to take a nap first, then we can go." he replied.

When he went to his room to nap, I began to wonder with much dismay of what might be going on with him and what symptoms he had voiced could mean. I began saying the 'Our Father' over and over to myself and asking God to keep Lance well. I felt my heart rate increase and then began to feel anxious. The 'Nervous stomach' set in.. Argh.. Oh how I really dislike to sit and wait when there is this unknown. Continuing to pray and struggling to focus on my quilt project I managed to keep going, but began foreboding the joy of this beautiful Sunday. I kept praying as I needed to kick this ugly feeling. I told myself "Just participate, do not anticipate. Its all in Gods hands." My gut started to settle a bit and I just kept praying. I noticed when I would stop praying the nervousness would increase.

About an hour later Dad walked down the steps to the living room area and the kids heard his voice and began running upstairs to the kitchen and said with great anticipation, "Can we go four wheeling now?" Dad replied, "I'll go if mom goes." With feelings of being overwhelmed- as I was working on a project of eight quilts that needed to be finished in five days- I reluctantly replied, "OK I'll go as long as you all help me finish unpinning all these quilts when we get back." Everyone agreed and all were very excited and anxious to get going. It was 5:20 pm when we were able to take off out of the yard on our adventure, oblivious of the life-changing tragedy lying ahead.

As we ventured out on the four Wheeler's we headed east on gravel roads. It was a beautiful Minnesota day with a shining sun and short-sleeve temperatures, and Lance was in the lead. As we took a break by a sand pile the boys took to just being boys and doing a little showing off. Lance asked me where I wanted to ride to next and I said "I would love to keep heading east towards the Ridge." This being one of our favorite rides which is about 3-4 miles east of our farm. It is the shore line of Minnesota's Lake Agassiz. Here the rolling hills and many lakes and ponds consume this beautiful land. We live in the Red River Valley so having everything flat and the ability to see for miles, therefore arriving in the rolling hills is quite a change in scenery.

As always Lance would continue to lead, with the kids in the middle, and me taking up the rear. We continued on for another four miles and we came up to the county highway, where we stopped and then we turned to the south. As I approached the turn I could see there was a problem ahead. My oldest son Levi was yelling frantically and waving at me, shouting, "Hurry up, it's Dad!! It's Dad". As I drove up the ditch to the highway I saw one ATV belly up and the other laying on its side. Sitting at the crest of a hill, I scrambled with the kids to remove the ATVs from the highway, fearing another accident. Levi then said to me, "Mom "I can't find Dad." I told him to just keep yelling his name and we would find him, trying to assure him that things would be okay. Levi and I continue to search the ditch and ditch-bank, which had very tall grass. All of a sudden Levi screamed, "Mom!!!! He's right here!!!" I ran to Levi and saw Lance. As he lay in a supine position, with his head tilted down towards the bottom of the ditch and his legs angled upward towards the road. He was bleeding from his head, and he was breathing, but unresponsive. I then instructed the boys to grab his legs and I would support his neck by holding him in C-spine. We crawled up the side of the ditch, holding his neck in place, and with all their strength they helped me get Lance up to the road. The boys were truly amazing. After Alex, the boys' friend riding with us, had called for emergency services, my nurse-trained instincts kicked into full. Lance was loosing much blood from his head so I instructed Levi to take my sweatshirt off which was tided around my waste and use it to apply pressure to Lance's head wound. Lance than began posturing. (this is an abnormal involuntary flex-ion or extension of the arm and legs which indicates a severe brain injury) It took all of us to hold him down. He did this several times. As I monitored his vitals I could feel his heart was still beating, his respiration's decreasing and other obvious signs presenting themselves which began to prepare me with the fact that his body was shutting down. At that moment of seeing my husband in his distress, my boys being strong, scared, and worried all at the same time; my resilience began to present itself. As the ambulance arrived I was asked to ride along, hesitate due to fear of the known that Lance's condition was grave, and that his wounds could be fatal, I did get into the rig. Listening in the back to the Paramedics having difficulty trying to intubate (placing a plastic tube into the trachea to keep an oral airway open) him, I started continually praying to myself. Saying the 'Our Father' and asking God to give Lance no more pain, no more suffering, and to assist the Medics with their challenging and difficult tasks.

Upon arrival to the nearest emergency Department, at Fergus Falls Regional Hospital, we were informed that a Life Flight helicopter was awaiting our arrival. Sitting as a passenger in the ambulance, I was asked to run the siren that means 'Get the heck out of the way!; Pull over!; I'm an ambulance trying to transport someone who is in a life and death situation!' That ere e sound and knowing the urgency of that moment sends a chill up my spine. Relieved that Lance was going to be taken 60 miles to a Trauma hospital with more specialists, Sanford Hospital in Fargo, It confirmed my suspicions that Lance was very seriously injured. The local hospital staff diligently worked to stabilize him for the flight, with so many people attending to him, you could not even see the gurney. As they moved toward the helicopter the flight medics asked if I would be riding with Lance. Worried about my kids and how they would get to Fargo, I declined and opted to meet them at the hospital.

As I emerged from the emergency room, Alex's mother, Karen, also a nurse, we were approached by the attending doctor. Tentatively explaining Lance's injuries and condition, Karen states "Cut the crap, we are both nurses and we understand what's happening." As he escorted us to a private room, I passed another room where

Lucas was being attended by a nurse. I then changed my direction and with much be-wilderness I looked at the nurse and said "what are you doing? What's going on???" Lucas arm was rapped in some gauze and she was cleaning another minor wound. I walked over to Lucas and said "you got hurt too?" Lucas Speechless, Levi then said "Mom, the 4 wheeler that was 'belly up' was Lucas'. He hit the tar due to Dad's 4wheeler was rolling out of control and there was no way Lucas could avoid it." That moment, helplessness consumed my body! My son got hurt and I didn't even know it! The strength Lucas used to assist his dad to the top of the road and he had an injured arm and wrist? I was sick to my stomach. Karen and I then proceeded with the doctor to another room where he gave Lance's complete status. The Glasgow Coma Scale was collected which is a tool that measures trauma to the brain and Lance's Glasgow Score was a 4. The lowest score possible is a 3. I was devastated.

My father and a sister met us at the hospital. As we drove to Fargo it occurred to me, and I expressed to all, that I didn't believe Lance would survive. As I watched the helicopter fade into the distance I continuously repeated the Lord's Prayer, and asked the Lord for strength for the kids and I, and comfort for our Lance.

Upon arriving at the Sanford hospital in Fargo I was greeted by my Mom, Morgan, and other family. Needing a change from my blood-stained clothes the nurse asked me if I wanted some scrubs to wear. I instinctively informed her I was a "medium" and she stated "you wouldn't happen to be a nurse would you?" I replied "yes Mam." As I changed, it occurred to me that I putting on nurses' scrubs, my husband was dying, and I'm 34 and would be raising three kids alone. I just prayed for continuous strength to remain calm for my kids.

The accomplished neurosurgeon working ER that evening was from Los Angeles, California. He was calm, experienced, compassionate and realistic. He informed me that Lance had suffered a stroke, the whole left side of the brain had been affected, and his brain stem was already turning black. He then told me that within a matter of hours his brain would completely hemorrhage and, then, he said, **"He will not make it."**

Strength!!! Purpose!!! Value!! Laughter!!! Smiles!!! Love!!!
Where the hell is it right now???

My only thought was that I had to see Lance. He was cleaned up very nicely and they had placed him on a ventilator. He was resting peacefully. His heart rate was good and his hand was nice and warm. I then went back to the waiting room and got Morgan as she had not yet seen him.

As i was bringing Morgan back to her dad I explained that he looked like he was sleeping but that he could hear us. I told her he had a white dressing over his head where he had a cut from falling off the four wheeler. But otherwise he was still our big tough guy.

After talking with the doctor and trying to understand the gravity of it all, I decided to visit with the kids. We finally had the time to determine what happened on that fateful ride. Lucas, who was riding behind Lance said, "It was really weird, Mom! All of a sudden dad stood up, braked, and then he veered off to the right and flew from the four-wheeler. The ATV was going all over the place until it flipped and I ended up hitting it and getting knocked off from mine." It turns out that this sudden stop was the result of a stroke, and there was not an accident with anyone who would have to bear that burden.

Later in the day now they moved my husband to a room in critical care and to our surprise they had placed a beautiful John Deere quilt on him as he rested quietly. There was something about this room that was very familiar to me. It was the room I was in when I had been in a very bad automobile accident in 2003. The only difference was my bed was bed one and Lance was in bed two.

It was at that point where these 'coincidences' as most people refer to them, but I call them God-given moments began. Up until this point I had been praying and asking God for strength of a different sort, and it was at that moment I realized I wasn't alone then, or in the future to tend to my duties as a wife, mother, and nurse. Naturally when one has some familiarity with their surroundings ability to be more at ease is present. Many friends and family arrived at the hospital, stories were told, tears and laughter were among the entire family waiting room. Though we could not see him the Great Almighty was holding all of us close to his heart!!!

Strength can be defined "as the quality or state of being physically strong, the ability to resist being moved or broken by a force, or the quality that allows someone to deal with problems in a determined and effective way." [1] Which definition would describe who you are to the one for all and then use it as a starting point basis to walk through your journey? It amazes me to see the three definitions as all of us have the ability to have at least one. Have you ever asked yourself how we got that strength? Well, my friend, we all have been given some extraordinary strengths that shape, describe, and characterized who we are. It is how we receive these strengths that will determine the Final Result. The reality of finding and maintaining strength I do not believe is even humanly possible to do on your own. Can One use resources to guide them and learn the grieving process and the different coping skills and how to adapt to change and maintain in life?....absolutely!!! But it seems so temporary. I need a very solid basis that I can easily step on without falling and have always, to continue being who I am and who I want to be. When I do things I always want to have a purpose for doing it....a meaningful purpose not something temporary and superficial.

Maintenance of our strength...this is far from a simple task, but remember **"all things are possible with the help of our great Almighty!"**

"But He said, What is impossible with men is possible with God." (Luke 18:27)

(Matthew 11:28)states "come to me all you that are weary and are carrying heavy burdens and I will give you rest." I used to believe strength correlated with being physically strong.....oh how experience quickly changed my thought process☺

Jessica Lyngaas

CHAPTER 3

Purpose and Value

Now despite all the commotion and medical uncertainties one thing was certain: Lance told me if he were to die he wanted to be a donor. So to help him achieve this goal I knew I needed to speak up and talk to the appropriate people. With everything happening so fast and furious this huge part of who Lance was became a huge reality, obviously much sooner in our lives than I was ready to interpret, accept, and accomplish. This moment in my life I needed to take control and make very clear and sound choices.

The staff at Sanford hospital began assisting me with the daunting process of organ donation. Knowing the amazing miraculous events that happen for some very ill people by donating a vital organ filled my heart with much love, joy, and self-worth. My purpose always has been to give... giving whatever it may be if given an opportunity. I thought to myself two things; the obvious "Lance is a donor and he is a man of his word, and the second was I too am a woman of my word and will not be hypocritical. Therefore I have life and so does he (Lance) thus we are not greedy so the decision was made.

The compassion and peace that comforted me was astounding. Near midnight, I was on the phone with a company that specializes in organ transplants, LifeSource. It was then I consented to the organ donation. Many questions and different feelings of doubt set in, but with continual prayer I made the decision I could and would not do this alone without guidance from Above.

Exhausted both physically and mentally, I needed to sleep before I physically collapse. My older sister, her daughter, Morgan, and I went across the street to the Scandi Hotel, which was for families who had loved ones in the hospital, knowing the nurse would call if Lance were to hemorrhage, or if any other drastic change would occur. Upon entering our hotel room there was a care package with different foods from Lance's employer-trust the Mid-westerners to be there with food in times of trouble.

Once I hit the pillow I was out and then just 45 minutes later I received a phone call. So, it was back to the hospital. Lance's pulse had shut up to 220. The nurses carefully explained what was occurring and showered all of us with tender care.

At that point Life Source was contacted and by seven the next morning the most gifted nurse I have ever met arrived on a jet from Minneapolis. As I saw this nurse coming down the hall and was told she was from Life-source. My inner feelings were "okay?" She is very young..." She introduced herself to me and I was thrown back.

That instant moment I began my journey of humbled astonishment. This young gal who was very much experienced in her role armed in this grim atmosphere with much poise and grace. Her ability to direct and coordinate not only the process of explaining organ donation to the family, but the attentiveness she exercised while interacting with her peers. This team was the nurses and doctors that were caring for Lance and whom were also going to be performing the 'Harvest of organs.' This truly was breathtaking. This nurse was not just a nurse with an awesome talent, this was a nurse whom had been given a gift from above. Her name was Megan.

She met with all the family and friends and gave her sincere condolences. She then provided an extensive explanation of what would happen next. This would be the end of Lance's physical journey, and the start of new life for others.

Friends and family then said their good-byes. *Not ready to leave the hospital I wanted to go see my Man before he started his new job of giving MORE LIFE. I say this with much expression, and not with anger, but with AWE...*

Not being able to even comprehend what had occurred or what was about to occur, I walked in Lance's room with my daughter and my sister, Joanna. One of the nurses offered to shut off his 'vest treatment' / lung simulator but I declined, knowing that the CPT helps keep the lungs viable.

Lance was comfortable and patiently awaiting his next assignment from Above.

Morgan and my youngest sister said goodbye. I then told them I would meet them down in the parking lot.

As I stood over Lance and held him with a hug I gave him a kiss and told him I loved him. Assuring him that all would be okay and that Id see him again in Paradise. Not wanting to give the nurse any eye contact I told her "thank you" and escorted myself out of his room. Many tears flowing down my face I observed other staff members with tears too along with silent expressions that showed love and, comfort, and compassion. As I exited that critical care floor and proceeded down to my sisters vehicle I realized I wasn't walking alone.....God was with me. He was there guiding me through each step I took....

We need only to open our eyes and ears to see and hear him. We are never alone. While we were saying our 'good byes' my sister and I observed an extremely gifted Sanford nurse. She had just began her shift and she quietly took orders of what medications and treatments she was to perform and she then began her duties. She explained everything to Lance before performing it. We knew he was in good hands.

I got into JoAnna's car and the two of us looked at each other and at the same time said. "Wow!!! I want to be as competent as that nurse was!!" With much amazement and with bittersweet feelings we both knew he was going to be okay.

After we left the hospital, we headed home and as we pulled into my farmyard the driveway was full of vehicles and swarming with people. I walked into the house to find our back room filled with bags and boxes of food, plates, napkins, and enough goods to feed a small army.

As I savored the aromas, and the love and condolences from so many, I knew that this was a true example of *"Minnesota Nice"*.

When you wake up each day do you ever wonder how or why you're at the position or place you are at in life, and anticipate what that day or future is going to bring-what your purpose might be on that day? I could never possibly have dreamed a purpose for this fateful day.

Purpose: "The reason for which something exists or is done, made, or used; An intended or desired result; end; aim; goal; Determination, resoluteness. The subject in hand; the point at issue. Practical result, effect, or advantage -to act to good purpose-"[1]

If you'll begin each day with fuel from Christ the miles you can go in one day are endless! like no other! I guarantee it! Laugh, doubt, or think this is ridiculous, that's all right, it's the truth! It works and it is so simple! If you read the prayer of Our Father... look and hear the third phrase...Thy will be done on earth as it is in Heaven... now read the definition of Purpose again. This simple task has amazed, comforted, and guided me time and time again through the decades to the point that it is my food and if I do not receive it I feel awful, ugly, and have much discouragement.

"Our father who art in heaven hallowed be thy name thy kingdom come, Thy will be done on earth as it is in heaven. Give us this day our daily bread and give us our trespasses as we forgive those who trespass against us and lead us not into temptation but deliver us from evil For thine is the kingdom and the power and the glory now and forever. Amen. (Matthew 6: 9-13)

Jessica Lyngaas

CHAPTER 4

Control

With so much to be planned for the funeral, the week was exhausting. Because Lance was a donor and it was unknown how long it would take to harvest his organs, the funeral was planned for Saturday June 18, 2011.

I appreciated the additional time to prepare. You see, any time we did a project, whether working on the house or chores for the farm it was always very fast, furious, and thorough. Lance was very meticulous and hardworking and believed if something was started it would be finished FIRST before we would go to the next thing.

So now that I was in control I decided the funeral was going to be planned with great detail and thoroughness and it was to be his grand finale. We also spent a great deal of time and effort into his wake service scheduled on Friday, June 17, our 16th wedding anniversary.

This particular weekend was also going to be the annual Keaveny Family Reunion and many family members were flying home for it. Much planning took place and the kids and I, family, and neighbors pitched in to help with having a beautiful final celebration for Lance.

The wake service was the beginning of the celebration of Lance's life. When I arrived at the church I was truly amazed. There was a John Deere combine, a Caterpillar tractor, two John Deere 'B' **tractors,** and many people. The reassurance of love and support was very obvious!!!

A couple hours before the wake service started I was given the message that three of Lances organs were given to one man; they consisted of his heart, liver, and a kidney. When given this information I was in awe for the amazing news, but anticipating reactions from friends/ family. Encountering people for the first time as the 'widow', well lets just say it consumed most of my energy.

Four priests and a deacon said Lance's Funeral Rites and other family members performed their talents with singing, speaking, and praising the Legacy that Lance was leaving here on earth. His uncle Jerry and Jerry's son Justin sang and let me tell you they can sing!!! The 'Our Father' was song by Justin acappella. He rocked that sanctuary! I can still hear him singing it and it sends chills up my spine! There was so much strength and meaningful emotion pronounced that I could feel the assurance from Above that all will be okay.

Uncle Jerry sang Go Rest High on that Mountain, and sang "Son go rest high on that Mountain, Lance your time on earth is done." Another song that was chosen was 'I am Well with my Soul'. Lance was well with his soul and he gave every last piece of life he could give. He really did! All the detail that took place was so memorable and was a complete depiction of who Lance was.

Little did I know what the future would hold at this point. I am always thrilled with Technology and medicine and now the ability One has to give life to someone else?!?!
I'm feeling so humbled.....God just keeps comforted me.

The following poem was read-at Lance's Wake Service.

The Lance I Knew

The Lance that I knew was a really great dad, he loved his wife and his children with all that he had.

The Lance that I knew would be called a "good old boy." as he joked with his family or described his latest toy.

The Lance that I knew was a hard working man, trucking nights on the road and working the land.

The Lance that I knew was a really great friend, who'd be there beside you till the very end.

The Lance that I knew cherished his wife, and will always be her soul mate even after this life.

The Lance that I knew was a dependable man, each call for help was answered with a simple, "yeah, I can."

The Lance that I knew loved to tease and to play, enjoying this life till his very last day.

The Lance that I knew, from God he was sent, and Full Throttle to Heaven he was called back and he went.

This poem explains who Lance was to a 'T'!!

{this poem was written by Amy Jungwirth. She is the wife of Steve who went to college with Lance. This couple is very near and dear to our family.}

Saturday came and in addition to the combine and Caterpillar and all the machinery out the front of the church, I also saw a beet truck and our friend Eric's huge charter party bus. These vehicles all were representation of Lance: the beet truck is the one he drove the previous winter hauling sugar beets for Min-Dak Farmers Coop; from the Caterpillar tractor he had planted corn that very spring; the combine was his ultimate thrill as a farmer; the party bus he often drove when needed.

The last thing we planned for the procession was to have a Black Ford F350 Diesel Crew Cab pickup. Lance and I had a Black 'Outlaw' Special Edition Ford F350 that we recently had sold and instead of having the Hurst take Lance to the cemetery, he was brought out in this pickup. This is what he would have wanted... He was a farmer! Hauling stuff around in pickups and trucks.

There were so many people, literally hundreds in the funeral procession out to the cemetery, and as we approached MN Highway 9, I turned to my left I could not believe what I saw: the crowd of people standing outside the church was like watching a funeral procession on TV of a celebrity that had just passed away.

The numbness that had set in continued, my emotions were humbled, my thought process became more thorough, and time was no longer going to be fast and furious... Only in a time of emergency was I going to all that pace.

To many things had occurred in my little 16 years of marriage... 34 years of Life. Many of which were completely out of my control. I'm a 'go-getter' and do not throw-in -the-towel! We are born into this world with an expiration date therefore will pass on through this life on earth. It is not only a fact it is a reality. Not only is it part of His plan, but I believe that as Lance shines down on all of us, he is able to see us growing into his ultimate crop of golden wheat.

This day of letting Lance go quieted my words and opened my heart completely to the Lord. After all my husband is now with the Maker and has no more pain, suffering, and can enjoy his Dad and farming with no worries and is surrounded by so much love!!

God is the Master, why not let him lead. I literally felt like he carried me around like a bird full of feathers as my 'wings' had been clipped. Though I felt weak, I didn't have the awful feeling of FEAR of the unknown any longer. This may sound a bit absurd, but it is the truth. I've been slammed down hard so many times and was able to get back up each time. This only because I had God in my life. At this time in my life I most certainly would not allow fear to control myself and kids.

I looked around and saw so many other single parents surviving. I could survive too. That was my goal and my destination.

We've all heard the message of "keeping our eyes wide open." Focusing on what God has in store for us and looking to the Heavens continually became my routine. Knowing this task would be difficult because society was larger then I. The fact is God is larger than society and He is far more of a reward for Eternity.

"He rescued us from the control of darkness and transferred us into the kingdom of the Son he loves" (Colossians 1:13)

CHAPTER 5

Choices

Our blest Redeemer, Ere he breathed, his tender, last farewell, A guide, A comforter, bequeathed with us to dwell. He came sweet influence to impart, a gracious willing guest, where he can find one humble heart wherein to rest. And every virtue we possess and every victory won, and every thought of holiness are his, alone. Spirit of purity and Grace our weakness, pitying see: oh make our hearts Thy dwelling place, and worthier Thee. {Our blest Redeemer by Harriet Auber}

My life has now opened to a new chapter. Now that there were so many decisions, and choices screaming out my name, major change was present. I no longer had my life partner present to help me in the decision-making process.

I remember being asked by someone if I still looked at myself as Jessica Lyngaas, Lance's wife?

Well that's a loaded question! I thought, okay...This is where I am at: I am 34 years old, just buried my husband, who is the father of my three kids, I am a 'working outside the home', and a mother who has been left out on the farm to take over all the same responsibilities. By the way our kids were not just kids, they were teenagers! Not just one but three!

I believe the answer was yes and is Yes! Nothing has changed except my stress level! Ha!! Taking control and taking control of my choices that were to be made became very crucial. I have three teenagers and I want to make darn sure they maintain their levels of respect for themselves and others. I am it! I have come to far to throw that away.

We all remember being a teenager. Growing up I was ridiculed by many and not just by other kids. I remember thinking "Treat others as you want to be treated." I practiced this and continue to. I can not imagine treating others the way I have been treated. But nevertheless I am not going to dwell on the past. Just keep marching forward. I am not and will not thrive in darkness!

When Lance and I got married one thing that I heard many times was "well we know who wears the pants in the family.... and it certainly isn't Lance!" Wow, impressive right? Teasing? I do not think so, but deliberate and intentional, Yes!! Such a bold statement! Truth, Lance was the dominant and authoritative One and we compromised on 98% of all decisions! An example of making choices; I have forgiven but obviously haven't forgotten these words or actions!

Making sound choices and teaching my children on my own was now the process to continue to carry out! It is critical and one of my 5 top goals to achieve! My children have always been my top priority. If you were to visualize a priority list this is what it would look like for me:

#1 God #2 My Children #3 My Spouse #4 Myself #5 My Home

I thank God everyday for my children. This entire process of becoming a widow would have been far worse if I didn't have the joy and reminder of how wonderful kids really are. I am quite aware also of the trials and testing a parent constantly goes through, but the love of a child outweighs it all!

I love kids and I know how difficult it is to go through all the changes as a teenager WITH the presence of both a mother and father; now all these changes are going to occur with the absence of someone so valuable to my kids? Imaging what our teenagers were going to go through without their dad brought much worry and concern. I was determined to KEEP ON KEEPING ON!!!!

WOOT! WOOT!!! Seriously is this really happening I thought to myself? Yeppers, Sweetheart, this is it!!! You've come to far and been through way more than you imagined so now is not and will not be the time to crumble! I had an awesome spiritual connection with God, so I thought...and then awesome became miraculous!

Daily surprising things would occur. Whether it would be words of Christ spoken through the lips of my kids or 'signs' that proved I wasn't here alone with these children. I constantly had a helping hand of guidance. I've always been one to go with my intuition and now began to realize this is GOD speaking to me!

How would I keep moving forward? I asked myself, "What do I have that has NOT changed? I thought first of **my faith.** That had to be my basis in life NOW! I just had to build on it!! I knew that I had to have consistency of choices, stand firm in my decisions, and strive daily to look to God for the strength to accomplish His will.

Knowing my minimal options brought me to the realization of how fast and furious our "little Lyngaas world' was. Slowing down and processing life was going to be a challenge. The only way I was going to get through theses 'bumpy road' state was with God and God alone!

Stop for a moment please and really think about this:

Think of all a person does in one day. Seriously its a bit ridiculous at times. Through all this busyness look around and really concentrate on what the core event/purpose that made this day go round. Sit and admire the beauty and creations that are looking at you constantly. It is unremarkable. And its all from God. We miss so much valuable time, people, words ... all because we really are to busy and do not take the time to enjoy what the Maker has created.

My three children know who I am and what I stand for. I lead by example, and I will continue to do so. Sometimes I must sound like a broken record, but repeating and teaching the kids consistency and how to make good choices is a full time job with unwanted overtime, and it is so rewarding to watch my kids grow and realize the dedication, consistency, and diligence that parenting has definitely paid off.

Standing firm is far from easy, actually often extremely difficult and is 100% worth the time and effort. The first month after Lance passed there was daily adjustments, sometimes even more, but life didn't stop here. It kept going and it became so fast that making sound decisions, taking time for myself and others had to be on my priority list.

As I walk through each day of life I have a choice to wake up and be happy or not. I realize circumstances that can occur during the day that will alter my feelings but if I tell myself that today is a good day I can praise God for His blessings.

I have my family, my job, my health, and I am in control of ME, my feelings, and the choices I am going to make. Granted, this can be difficult, but if we Surround ourselves with distractions, negativity, and unproductive decisions; making good, sound choices can almost become impossible. It is like entering a smoke-filled room..... It is hard to see, breath, and it is very toxic to your body.

Daily I make a choice to be only in a POSITIVE frame of mind. How do I do that? I start each of my mornings with scripture, prayer, sunshine, visits with my kids, and a plan for the day of how I'm going to motivate and fulfill the purpose God has for me.

Fill your cup with faith, hope, and love in the morning, your mind and body are energized with positive, motivating spirit that will get you through your day and help you overcome obstacles that may fall in your path. By the time the day is over, your cup will only be partially emptied, because God stays at your side and will not let you be depleted. :)

This marked a road sign on my map of life....I have made the choice that I will never take anything for granted. I will not lose my Faith in our creator. I find it troubling when I observe those who think they have the upper hand and they are in control. While we can control our choices we make, we do not necessarily have control of circumstance that can be life-changing.

What are you going to do when you wake up every day and make your choices?

"Because God satisfied the one who was parched with thirst, and he filled up the hungry with good things!" (Psalm 107:9)

{jot it down ☺}

CHAPTER 6

Coping mechanisms

Tackling life with my kids and continually encouraging them to see the joy in our events that have occurred and will continue to occur became second on my priority list. Focusing only on 'Light', meaning positive issues. As the four of us had daily stressors, much effort of trying to normalize these feelings and thought process's continued through our detail of a Life. It also became much less of a hindrance each and everyday. Though very difficult some days, we were always able to see the joy that each day can bring us.

Alert and aware of the toxicity that can poison One real fast, especially when that person is down on love and in Faith of God, brought me to a solid platform here on earth. Reflecting back in time, many lessons have been taught through trials.

When I was forced to lay for four months in a halo. 'Cope' became my middle name. Patient? No patience! This was months of many learning skills. I wasn't the caregiver anymore. I was the one cared for! What? This sucks!! I'm a nurse, and furthering my education!! What in the heck is going on?

I remember my boss from the home care agency I worked for coming out to the house to admit me for Home Care... Ohhhh ... NOT COOL!!! This is not really happening is it?

I had it all planned. I was going to have my Home Health Aide drive me to class at the college and then I would have to do my clinical hours as a n RN student after I came out of wearing my halo. My Boss/RN Case worker said "Jessica, a month has passed. The program had to dismiss you due to your accident and medical issues. You no longer have a spot in the RN program."

Devastated to say the least, I didn't want to hear this. My brain was fine! It is just my body! Frustration and anger set in! I only had seven months left and I would be done with the program!! Why Why Why!!!! I remember thinking Who do these people think they are? Dismissing me from the RN program. I never signed anything! I was a great student and hadn't done anything wrong!

Reality definitely was thrown up on me that moment!! When you have put so much determination, consistency, and hard work into your career and then it is thrown out from under you?!?! Argh! Argh! Argh!

This was a major point in my life where I had to cope and deal with not just one situation but several! There was no other options! I struggled for quite a while with this, praying hard and always trying to find the positive and to stay focused!

As long as I had my children around I could see great reason to move forward and work hard at getting stronger (physically and mentally). There was nothing more healing then my kids coming up to me and hugging me and saying "I love you Mom!"

Because I was a Home Health Nurse and supervised home health aids, I was given the opportunity to choose my aids. I only picked the finest! Their time and abilities brought me through my duration of dependence on many, and much pain physically and emotionally.

When a person comes to this point in life. Life becomes very difficult to grasp, but understanding life and focusing your eyes Above becomes real simple...*I will lean on God for it all. If the mindset is "I want it now God!!... well unfortunately it probably will not occur.* I believe with all my heart that God has a plan for all of us and I accept that. "It is all in God's timing" Really concentrate on this message.
(I Peter 5:6)

Learning to cope is hard no matter the circumstance. I certainly never anticipated losing my husband this early in life. Too often, people rely on themselves as they process their thoughts. Allowing pride and feelings of strength that are beyond human abilities becomes more of a battle field then a benefit. We need others and others need us. Think about the chain of life. Unfortunately, some may not cope and they become very judgmental and opinionated, lose their faith, and immerse themselves in negativity, then end up creating negative chaos and living with heartache and pain.

As I grew up I was taught to have respect for others, especially your elders. Never to be selfish or consider yourself the center of attention or to be greedy. Instead, giving of yourself when able, and being a good, Christ-like example. These foundations have shaped my values defining who I am and what I continue to stand for.

These valuable lessons too have been passed on to my kids. Coping tools for me include keeping things familiar, consistent, and staying close with my children. Keeping Christ close in my daily walk and sharing it with others and having no apprehension to speak the Word.

Earlier I mention the negative chaos or noise that becomes prevalent in so many families after death. I cannot speak for everyone but perhaps many, but all the 'noise' in our world really distracts what

God intended for us. God wants us to be loving, giving, and praise him. Chaos isn't always a bad issue, but when it is looked at or becomes just routine and not brought to ones awareness and it is used as an example or tool to learn from, then it is negatively understood.

(Romans 8:35-39) "expresses how God never separates us from his love and no matter the circumstance we need to cling to him in time of need." Lord knows I know this to well! I'm clinging to him and not letting go!!! I can't! Its a brutal world we live in!!

It is hard to verbalize the thoughts and feelings and help your children differentiate emotions when internally you are right there struggling with that exact emotion. This is where BALANCE becomes your best Advocate.

Through many frustrations, tears, and laughter I began to utilize this resource. Realization of this way of life is possible because anything is possible with the Will of God. Honestly if I do not focus on the day and really put Christ in the center and have that balance I struggle! Oh how I struggle.

I've recognized that the number one issue that interferes with my 'balance in life' is the fact I like to please people and seek their approval. I didn't think this is who I was but when I have sat down and evaluated the situation, this was my conclusion. What a challenge and sometimes a failure that I had set myself up for! How can I change this? I NEED TO PUT GOD FIRST....WITH EVERTYHING!!

I've adapted to many changes as many do. My physical health has began to challenge me in many areas since my accident in 2003. In 2010, I was diagnosed with Celiac Disease. For those who do not know what this is it is when One is allergic to Gluten. Gluten is in everything or at least that is the way it felt when I was diagnosed.

Changing my diet intake, not to mention changing your spending habits on food was Life changing! Not only did I have to sit back and watch people eat scrumptious food I also had to constantly be asked "Oh, are you a picky eater?" I would reply "No!, actually I love food and could eat anything if able!" I then would get that look of be-wilderness from the questioner. I later learned to respond in a more polite manner.

After all I always have been good at explaining myself. Ha! Constant frustration and discomfort soars through me! I am not going to let any of this medical stuff slow me down or take my joy away from where I am at and who I am here in this life.

Maintaining coping skills for everyone is very important. There are so many areas where we as humans have to cope. It works in alignment with our critical thinking abilities. If we do not cope, the event at hand keeps poking and prodding at our everyday living; every moment breathing. You do not have to forget the reality of the issue, but forgiving the action is necessary!

Since Lance has passed, the emotional pain and hurt that I had and still have is something I would never wish upon anyone. I also believe that 90% of it could have been, and can be, absent or avoided. Sometimes hurting people end up hurting people due to the the hurting that was not dealt with through proper coping mechanisms for the other hurting person.

We are human and we do not have magical powers to fix or change others, and we all will and do cope differently and that is good and OKAY. This is how God made us. We have all heard the scripture "treat others as you want to be treated". This is really a powerful statement from the Bible. I believe when a person is so rude and unkind to another human or any creature of God, they are internally fighting a huge battle.... ALONE!

Perhaps its jealously, insecurity, poor self-esteem, or self image. Whatever the issue may be, understand that we are all created by God's hands and when we begin to try to destroy one with hurt, doubt, and much discouragement realize who your actually directing the destruction to...Christ!

Some ideas to help show love and support for All to try when involved with One who is coping after death and that may also help prevent negative chaos include; respecting their feelings and choices (even if you disagree with it and also as long as they are not a threat to themselves or others) and respecting their ability of making choices. After all they are not deceased; their loved one is.

You cannot expect them to think and react to situations as they had in the past. Within each day that comes and goes for the survivor there is a common feeling of emptiness that is screaming, "GONE!!! EMPTY!!! YOU'RE ALONE NOW!!! "Yep, we are aware our loved one is gone. We will not forget it especially because every hour that goes by through the day there are constant reminders of our loved one." While we try to move forward or step out of the normal routine to cope, each day is going to be different! There is one less person involved in our life on a daily basis.

Because God has created us all so different he gave us personalities different then our fellow neighbor. This doesn't give us the right or the ability to make negative judgment calls regarding the way One is coping just because their way is not your way. I apologize for those who may interpret this as criticism or find these words abrupt, but instead insight into how to assist those coping with loss or just with life in general.

Words can absolutely destroy One, and they can also build and nurture! Please, please, please always think before you speak!! None of us hold the 'Master Book' to another human, therefore understand we do not have the capability to tell others how to think, feel, or act! We are all different!

"Be well balanced, be vigilant, and cautious at all times; for that enemy of yours, the devil roams around like a roaring lion, seeking someone to seize upon and devour." (I Peter 5:8)

CHAPTER 7

Doubt and Anger

It's amazing how these two little action words can really 'cramp your style'! (doubt and anger) One of the most frustrating things or I guess My One thing that annoys me the most in life is when I am doubted, whether with a decision I made or a statement. When you doubt someone or question another it gives the other person a sense of uncertainty, a decrease in confidence, and a loss of motivation, self-worth, and value.

Beginning life after a major change in One's health, job, or a loss due to death there are so many uncertainties and many unknowns that become part of your daily routine. Naturally you feel less of value and your self-worth and confidence and motivation are all decreased or sometimes absent. Therefore when somebody is trying to continue on through life especially after death it is very important to be considerate and think before you speak. Like my kids always will say

"You watch your own bobber (a fishing lure)."

One piece of wisdom that I pass on to my kids regularly and have since they were young is this: "Remember, you are solely responsible for your words and your actions. Always be mindful of what you say or do and realize what the result can do to an individual."

I believe people doubt others due to fear or the desire to be 'in control', or maybe because the other person has less experience than the doubter. Whatever the case marking your words is a lesson we all should apply in our daily life.
{Jesus explains this in (John 21:18.)}

As I had become doubted by some I felt my Joy was being stolen. I felt I was constantly having to justify my every word and action. The love drained right out of my heart. This was so miserable.

I think back of a few situations where I processed 'my plan' for several months. I then made a clear and sound decision. Not only was this decision making process time consuming but it was very much mentally difficult. This decision became a devastating and unplanned chaotic disaster. All because I allowed others to doubt me!

I listened so obediently to the pure selfishness and insecurity that flowed like a river drowning out a field. It overflowed its 'banks' After time elapsed and the 'water went down', the after math left a picture of ugly, dead, and lifeless array.

This doubt led to so many feelings of anger. My joy was depleted and my anger became so powerful. Frustration set in and I felt incapable of making decisions, worrying about doing or saying 'wrong things' because the fear of upsetting others was going to be much more destructive then the actual word or action at hand.

I would pray about it and keep doing my daily routine which had brought me thus far and then I had a huge eye opener and was able to see what was occurring and also what I was allowing to happen to myself and my kids.

I know our Lord Jesus Christ had his hand on all of us and he wouldn't let us out of his sight. I had always made good sound choices, advocated positively to my children through love and nurturing and provided love, respect for others including myself.

This toxic environment wasn't going to happen! I was a joyful, happy, loving person and I still continue to be. I can not allow negativity in to ruin what I have diligently established for years!! I own this!! The Lord Jesus is my founder and keeper!! Anger is not and will not be a seed that will be planted on my property!!!

Having and recognizing negative thoughts after a loss is normal and is a natural process. Making the choice of either indulging in the negative and remaining there or accepting the situation and moving forward in a positive manner.

All of these choices will occur in your own and good timing. No rush. Take your time and process. Do not allow others to make or doubt your decisions. You own it and you are free to be you!

This anger I was having was not directly related to the death of my husband. Though it exploded because Lance was no longer there! It was many years of on going words and actions from influencers' that felt the ability to make decisions for my children and myself. It was at that time of rationalization that this control was causing wounds and needed to be released so we could heal.

When somebody expresses their opinion, it can be presented angrily. One may not necessarily be able to pinpoint with whom they are angry at or at what they are angry about. In most cases the ones that are most close to that person end up receiving the blunt of their anger.

Because of this even more destruction and unhealthy situations begin. There are so many unknown answers of why we lose a loved one. Really we do not lose them as we know where they are, they are in Heaven, they are not lost. Hold this belief and trust it!

We question many areas in our life and naturally become upset. We are human. We want to know why? It seems we always have to be moving our lips and getting answers and busily flying through our day. This is the 'norm' for our society.

One thing I have learned very quickly is that if I can humble myself and sit quietly, it is amazing the messages that I hear my heart tell me. It is then I am able to savor the beauty that surrounds me.

We, as individuals, can manage doubt and if we have the right tools and resources. One simple tool and resource that most of us have is the Bible of our great and almighty God. We all can succeed, but we cannot do it alone. This truth is real and simple: we need God in our life in order to succeed upward and in a positive direction. He is amazing and always good.

Another is our heart. Allow your heart to be your guide through this journey on earth. It can provide a clear direction when you are lost. I was told by a very dear friend many years ago "Follow your heart Jessica. If it's soft and smooth go with it! If its scratchy, don't do it!" Believe me this saying has been rewound several times in my head and applied to many of my decisions.

One other thing you can do if your stubborn like me and do not feel like pulling out the Bible and reading the Good Word or if your too anxious to listen to your heart, get outside and look to the Heavens. Look at the clouds and the trees. Listen to the birds or see the wildlife. The fresh air you breath, the beauty at your sight, and sounds of peace will encompass your every cell. All of it is created by the Magnificent.

I will go out and take pictures of the clouds, trees, sun. What you see with the naked eye is way different then what the camera captures. I have so many awesome photos with amazing results like none other.

Do you remember hearing the scripture, "You are never alone. I am with you always.?" Well guess what? It is so true! Physically you may be home alone or driving by yourself but God is constantly around you and guiding you. The problem is we don't always take the time to recognize His presence.

After Lance died the one very strong feeling I had was my heart aching with pain. The pain could be compared to when your stomach is empty and you are starving because you have not eaten. Now multiply that pain many times over and realize that it doesn't just go away with food and it will continue for an unknown amount of time.

Those of you who have suffered a loss of a close loved one can comprehend this pain of which I speak. When I finally made up my mind that I could not face this pain alone, and when I "filled my cup with Scripture and devotion with God each morning that empty 'hole' became filled and my pain tapered away, not completely gone, but bearable.

You see that was the realization that I had not prioritized my duties correctly. The coolest thing about our Lord Jesus Christ is that when we 'get off track' he stands back and waits for us to 'get back on track' no questions asked.

May you find the strength and courage to start managing yourself. I know you can do it! All you have to do is start. What are some things you will do to conquer your anger and the feeling of being doubted?

**"When the Spirit of Truth comes, he will guide you in all Truth."
(John 16:13)**

CHAPTER 8

Acceptance

I've been excited to elaborate on this truth. Acceptance is the name of the game! With everything that happens in life and all the situations that we are placed in, how do we get through it? We can both remain silent and miserable and make others miserable or we can accept, go with it, and live a life of knowing God has a plan!

Recapping my life, it can sound quite complicated, but I do not interpret it that way. I look at it as this is what God had planned. This is what makes life so interesting and mysterious.

Since 2003 many areas of physical health continues to complex me. My neck (cervical spine) which already had a fusion in the upper area, now has a plate in it (and not one we serve food on), a cadaver bone, and 4 screws in the lower part of the cervical spine.

This all because the vertebrae decided to take charge and pinch a nerve for to long of a time, which then left my right hand with anger and much damage. Through many sessions of physical therapy and loss of my fine motor skills, neck surgery and then shoulder surgery followed each other. The end result was good and bad. I no longer had the extreme pain, but the damage was done and then lymphedema in my hand, arm, shoulder, and upper torso occurred.

This is very annoying to deal with. Everyday I have to wear compression on my hand, arm, shoulder and then a compression garment on my upper torso. It would be comparable to 'ted hose stockings' for the lower extremities, except this is for the upper part of the body. Wrapping my arm with special compression wraps at night also is necessary to prevent swelling and more circulation issues.

I also have a 'vest treatment' to utilize everyday. This is a unique machine that has 30-40 chambers in it and through light massage it pushes the fluid up and out of the body. The treatment takes 60 minutes to do. This will be a life time issue to wrestle with.

Pity party? Absolutely not. Only facts to help you visualize that life happens and many things will occur that are out of our control. If we do not accept these challenges, where does it lead us?

When I reflect on certain areas in my life that are frustrating. It is due to either myself not accepting or because others do not accept. This sounds maybe ridiculous to some, but think about this statement: when we decide not to accept something, we become negative about that situation. Yes? Therefore when the situation is brought up and we have our mind set in a positive direction, but then our influencing peers do not look at it in a positive way, we then can become swayed negatively and do not accept.

I'm not one at all to point the finger. I take full responsibility for my words and actions. This is an example of how we need to have our eyes and ears wide open and vigilantly focusing on what we see and hear from Above and not with what just surrounds us. There is a wide range of choices relating to acceptance, but many do not take the time to recognize it.

Since Lance passed, I get up every day looking for the positive, accept the circumstance, and move forward. Sound to good to be true? It is not! Trust me, I realize this is difficult, but it's actually easier to accept than to fight the truth.

This is where accepting the fact that God has a plan for each and every one of us and following his plan will result in a more productive and happy life. Do I have areas of interference? Yes, I do! Not only do I maintain myself but I also am continually shaping and guiding my two sons and my daughter.

Can you imagine what children would end up thinking or believing if their parents did not accept God's plan for their life? Would they be happy? As you may have heard, "If mama isn't happy, no one is going to be happy!" And truth is, the same applies to fathers.

Is one person seriously capable of managing three little brains that are not even fully developed, all the while managing thought process of their own and still have constant positive results? I don't think so. We need God to guide us and take control. After all he created us and everything that surrounds us.

So what is our human nature? "We all want to be in control." We want to make our own decisions. We want things to happen just the way we want them to happen. Well I am oh, so, very sorry to say that this way of thinking will not happen and if it does it is very short-lived and superficial.

How do you begin the accepting process? I believe the first thing is to accept yourself for who you are. God created you and if you really think about the magnificence of our minds and bodies, their tremendous capacities, you can realize that you are truly dignified. If you accept the way you look, feel, and where you are at here on earth, you're in agreement with yourself and in God's will you can be more settled and content.

Did you know we are all wired differently? It is okay that we are different than others. This is how God made us. Comparing One to others plays a big role in how one learns how to accept. Initially the individual needs to be at peace with how they look, live, make decisions, and be in agreement with what God has in store for them. Comparing who they really are to some other individual actually can rob a persons joy, self-esteem, and self-worth.

This piece of accepting contributes much to our World of constant HATE! We may not be able to fix the world, but we can shape ourselves and try to 'mold' into a Christ-like example. It all starts within our very own mind and body. *Listen to your heart......*My mindset of understanding that 'God has a plan for all of us' is what I have began to believe with all my heart and soul. I am determined to live by this -no questions asked!

Lance's death has helped me be encouraged to live in harmony with our Lord. Instead of wrestling around and living 'independently' I have decided to jump in the Co-pilot seat and allow God to take the YOKE.

This yoke is in control of my attitude. As my attitude rises in a positive and upward direction I am in collaboration and parallel with my Almighty'. This is much easier! Do I struggle with doing so? Yes, some days...But each day is a new day to begin a fresh start. What are some areas in your life or things about yourself that you are going to change so you can become in acceptance of who your are and where your at in life?

"But the Lord said to Samuel, Look not on his appearance or at the height of his structure, for I have rejected him. For the Lord sees not as many sees; for Man looks on the outward appearance, but the Lord looks on the heart." (I Samuel 16:7)

CHAPTER 9

Embrace

Each new spring, with the anticipated planting, and the resulting summer and fall harvest gave purpose to Lance. His Bohemian and German bloodlines provide him a strong-will and a punctilious nature: this drew me to him along with the fact that he was tall, dark, handsome-not to mention his buff physique. A true farmer and gentlemen, he thrived on teaching good values to his children through hard work, recreation such as fishing hunting, and the joy of spending time with loved ones. This was his purpose on this earth. He embraced it.

There has been so much change in the last 5 years, most of it still unbelievable. Lance was a donor and he still lives on. Our history is quite unique and has been bittersweet and is a remarkable story. We were soon to find out how Lance's life continued living on in others.

It was July, about a month after Lance died, when LifeSource called to check on the kids and I. They also shared that Lance's donation led to medical history. For the 11th time in US History, a recipient had received three organs from one person and then was able to donate an organ to a second person, becoming both a recipient and a donor.

They were also seeking my permission, if I would allow Lance's donation to be a a national story. At that moment, trying to gather my thoughts and realize what truly was occurring, and what was about to occur was overwhelming.

I knew I needed to consult with my kids and we were all in agreement that we should participate in sharing these remarkable events. I returned a phone call to LifeSource explaining that we were on-board, and added that we would like to meet the recipient and his wife.

This process of introducing myself and allowing the recipient and I to come to terms of the miraculous event that had taken place. Death and now life. The staff involved from LifeSource were very 'gifted' individuals.

Step by step the process to help prepare both the donor family and the recipient family was initiated. I was first encouraged to write a letter to the recipient and express who the kids and I were, and then who Lance was. This letter was sent to a couple different recipients and was also given to Golden Harris out of Chicago, IL, and NBC's Today Show in New York City.

The letter read as follows:

My thoughts on this entire journey of organ donation is far beyond my imagination at this point. Lance always was a donor and encouraged others to do the same. Everyone that knew him....know how strong he was both physically and mentally. He was very healthy and took pride in all he did.

With this whole amazing process of Lance being part of this domino transplant and knowing the rarity absolutely AMAZES ME!!.... Everything Lance did he did it 120% and if he couldn't do it 120% he would just assume not do it.

With this now occurring I think to myself... "Yep this is Lance... he doesn't just do a little...he does a lot." Lance was a Great Man who was full of strength, compassion, love, and support.....

I have been able to continue on my daily journey as a mother with a feeling of huge strength and faith that is beyond words. It's like I can hear him cheering me on to give at least 100%. It is such an honor to be part of this Awesome Encounter of Giving.

As a nurse it too sparks many thoughts of how many miracles doctors are able to perform and then to be part of one. When I think of the recipient who received three major organs from Lance, I am just in awe of how the gift of giving is so wonderful....

Life is so precious and to know that Lance's heart is still beating makes me feel so good. It gives me courage to continue with the same 'beat' I have always had and to be strong, loving, kind, and to give.

With everything tragic that occurs...there usually is something good that comes out and to just know that Lance's legacy continues on and will continue on....it is a reminder for me to live each day as if it were my last, to appreciate each moment I have with my friends and family, and to always be encouraged with what the Good Lord has planned.

We married June 17, 1995 and began our journey through life as husband and wife. We were blessed with a son Levi in 1996, another son, Lucas in 1997, and then a daughter, Morgan in 1998.

We grew fond of each other even more through the years. Lance was always a very giving person who never took rest. He enjoyed helping others, working hard, and making memories with his family. Family time was top on his list. We had a strong commitment to each other and I never had to worry he always provided.

Lance was never afraid to do more then what was expected. He loved to visit and could visit with anyone. Guarantee if someone new met Lance that day, they now became a new friend. He was a great example for all. He respected everyone, taught many, and encouraged those who needed encouragement. He was a wonderful teacher. From the basics in life to the tough struggles that many have to go through. Besides farming, Lance enjoyed fishing, hunting, snowmobiling, 4 wheeling, and just making memories.

Our oldest son, Levi, works very hard like his dad. He works at an airport for a crop duster and fuels the plane with jet fuel and chemical. He also has a farmer he helps with in the spring, harvest time, and fall.

Lucas, our second child, was his dad's little side kick. He too loves to farm and is very capable of much. He works for the Farmer my husband worked for, doing spring and fall tillage, combining, running grain cart, and also has a gifted talent of being a mechanic.

Morgan was 'daddy's little girl'. She is very studious, as was her dad. Lance always made time to cook, bake, or be her play mate. That was always the neatest thing to watch. She enjoys quilting, sewing, shopping, and her dad would always be right alongside her, always tending to her needs. Lance taught all of his kids what truly is important in life and I know these truths will always live on in them.

I am a nurse and enjoy helping and caring for others, probably good reason why Lance and I got a long so well. We have a strong faith and totally believe that our Maker always has the last say and he will provide. We enjoyed growing together and raising our children.

I could have never asked for anything more. We were parenting partners, each of us taking part cleaning the house, cooking the meals, and always making time for family. We never had a 'dull' moment. Humor and abundant laughter surrounded each of our days together. Lance was very quick-witted and could always bring somebody out of the 'blues'.

When I look now at all he did and has done...and is continuing to do: this is Lance... He didn't rest...and has now given more life. I have always been so proud of my husband for all his acts of kindness, not being selfish, and his huge gift of always giving.

I am so honored as his wife to be able to write to you right now and know that his gifts will continue to grow and provide life for you and your family. He has left a huge Legacy for all.

Sincerely,

Jessica Lyngaas

Time continuing on and trying to normalize our path here on earth became extraordinary and stamped daily with God's hand print. It was now August 2011 and I received a phone call from LifeSource and was informed my letter was received by the recipients and that the gentleman that received Lance's heart, liver, and kidney wanted to call me.

With much nervousness I agreed anticipating what the conversation would consist of. A few days past and one evening I received the phone call. On the other end of the line was the most delightful voice. The lady said "Jessica?" I said "yes, this is she." "My name is Rita Watson and I am Kirk's wife, the gentleman that received your husbands organs.."

With much relief, peace filled my body. I knew right away this woman was gentle, kind, and beautiful both inside and out. Her words were so comforting and I could feel my shoulders drop as the tension started to vanish.

She then put me on speaker phone and I was able to talk to both Kirk and Rita. After our conversation I remember thinking to myself. This has to be so difficult for them to call and talk to me.

Compare it to when you go on your first blind date or being interviewed for a new job ... The anticipation of the unknown words that will be said, etc... It felt like that. Now this conversation was taking place because someone had died. Only with the Grace of God did we carry on with joy and laughter. Time progressed and October came.

I was in Duluth, Minnesota, when to my surprise, I received a phone call from LifeSource. I was asked if I wanted to meet the recipient who received Lance's organs. This encounter would take place in New York City on national TV.

"WHAT?? IS THIS REALLY HAPPENING???" If I wanted to proceed with this gathering I would be receiving a phone call from a producer from the TODAY show --IN New York.

Oh my goodness!!! This was a call I never imagined receiving. I explained I would talk to my kids and get back to them on what our decision would be.

Speechless, amazed, excited, overwhelmed, nervous, sad; you can't believe the feelings that swallowed my mind and body during that phone call.

We returned home that evening and the next day I called LifeSource and told them we were ready and willing to meet the recipient. That very afternoon I received a phone call from the producer from TODAY.

We visited for about 25 minutes. With my heart full of excitement, and also much grief as we recounted Lance's death and organ donation. We then made arrangements for the producer to come to our farm for a family interview, and on the following day the kids and I would fly out to New York City.

This is crazy.... Someone is coming to my farm who is from NEW YORK CITY and she is going to interview the kids and I? OMG OMG!!! Somebody pinch me please because I seriously can not believe what is happening.

I contacted my advocate from LifeSource and explained the agenda and she asked if I would like to have her come to the farm when the interview took place and also if I would like her to come to New York with us. I told her "absolutely, I very much would appreciate it." The next day came and now it is November 2, 2011. The producer flew into Fargo and then drove down to our farm of rural Campbell. Her name was Kari. The most sweet and talented young 'New York-er arrived at the Lyngaas Farm.

Kari interviewed myself, asking many questions, and I shared many stories of Lance and my life together. As she ended her visit, she filmed the kids and I as we drove off from the farm on our four-wheelers.

Reflecting back this only occurred because of the Grace Of God! Wow this was awesome!!! Several different moments of silence I would hear the Good Lord speaking to me as I packed up our suitcases and prepared for the four of us to go to New York. This bittersweet occasion was happening and preparation was less and less. Not only was this our first time to New York it also was THE FIRST WEEKEND of DEER HUNTING!

Anyone in Minnesota that is an avid hunter knows this is Truly an important time of the year. We hosted the first weekend of deer hunting and this was our 16th year of doing so. On the top of the priority list for my boys this was going to take place and they were going to be out hunting that Saturday morning!!! Absolutely, I truly would not want this Holiday to be disturbed anymore than it was already going to be.

The next morning the kids and I flew to New York City to LaGuardia airport. We were instructed that, upon our arrival, a chauffeur would be there waiting for us holding a sign saying 'Lyngaas'.

Wow!! What an adrenaline rush!! NBC had a chauffeur there to pick us up. We were escorted out to a beautiful black Cadillac Escalade. Each of us quiet, nervous, and excited. We looked in awe at all the people, traffic, and the huge, tall sky scrapers.

The city was beautiful. Our chauffeur took us to our hotel and little did we know what beauty was awaiting us. We arrived at the Essex House, right across the street from Central Park. OMG!!! When we walked into the hotel we saw this huge, shimmering, crystal chandelier. It was gorgeous.

Everyone was very friendly, helpful, and kind. We were escorted to the check-in area and then greeted by an employee holding a warm plate with warm washcloths and the employee asked if we wanted to "freshen up". Feeling very much out of my element, I took the wash cloth and wiped my hands and said "thank you.".

I looked at my kids and Lucas said "Huh? You know what Dad would've done if somebody walked up to him holding a plate of warm wash cloths?" I giggled and said "Yes, I do know what he would've done!" The conversation continued to the elevator and laughter filled the air with the Lyngaas crew standing out like a sore thumb. I walked behind my kids with feelings of pride, accomplishment, commitment, and dedication as I observed all three of them walking through this breath-taking hotel.

It was November and it was cold, and my boys were dressed in their camouflage Rocky Mountain winter coats, Red Wing steel-toed work boots, and John Deere caps, not exactly typical New York attire. Morgan was in her beautiful black and white wool long coat, hobbling along due to she was in a walking cast from a high ankle sprain and hair line fracture in her foot/ankle. Joyfully, I observed the confidence in these three magnificent kids. They were content and accepting of this whole, entire situation. They were accepting of who they were and even in a city of 8 million people. They stood tall and proud of who of themselves and their roots.

When you can stand among people, particularly your own children, who are comfortable, real, and do not try to be something they are not, it is truly relaxing and becomes glorious. The boys were so good about helping Morgan. They carried her stuff and were constantly making sure I was doing well, too. I was and still am so proud of all of them. Observing the values and qualities that were implanted in them was so wonderful. It was a moment of gratitude that the constant teaching was being applied to their daily life.

Once we got up to our room I was to call the local radio station back home in Wahpeton, North Dakota as they wanted to interview me. Another new experience for myself and exciting. As the interview began all of a sudden I started receiving several text messages from people back home. It was at that moment I knew I had made the right decision and needed to really embrace the new beginning of what lye ahead. The love and support that the four of us received during the duration of experiencing New York was so inspiring.

Embrace the change that you encounter on this journey and then take that change and make it a positive part of your everyday life. In (Isaiah 3:18-21) God promises if we walk with him he will guide us and that we can expect good things both here on earth and in heaven.

"To grant to those who mourn in Zion – to give them an ornament of beauty instead of ashes. The oil of joy instead of mourning, the garment of praise instead of a heavy burden, and failing spirit. That they may be called oaks of righteousness, the planting of the Lord, that He may be glorified." (Isaiah 61:3)

CHAPTER 10

Hope

People always say "I hope the best for you". "I hope it all turns out OK." "Just be hopeful."

Do you ever just stop and really consider what do they mean? I have learned that when you hear that word of 'hope' from someone usually that individual has experienced something significant and they believe with their whole heart that good things can and will happen if you put your faith in hope.

My Hope: when we arrived to New York was that our introduction to Kirk, Lance's organ recipient, and his wife would be amazing, and absent of all feelings of confusion and awkwardness. Too, that my kids and I would be accepting and capable of meeting this man with open hearts beaming with warmth and love. This was a huge inhumane 'HOPE'. I knew my kids and their life was already different and awkward. Hope for peace was my wish and I placed my wants in God's ever so gentle hands.

Our New York adventures began and started in Chinatown. The kids wanted to try authentic Chinese food. We walked a few blocks and got onto the subway. Ooh, my! This was a new and a very fun experience for us all! Once we got off the subway we had the most amazing Chinese food. I don't think it can be any finer than this.

We then rode the subway to Time's Square. By this time it now was dark and New York City was even more spectacular: the lights and people, it was just amazing. We visited a few shops and then headed back to the hotel thinking it would be smart for all of us to shower that night versus waiting till morning.

Our plan was to meet our host from LifeSource at 7 AM down in the lobby and then wait for the chauffeur. We ordered room service that evening as we were all very hungry by the time we returned to the hotel. All exhausted, to say the least, we all showered, ate and then went to bed. As morning came and I woke up to Lucas rubbing my arm, saying "mom it is 6:45 AM."

I sprang out of bed and then we all jetted around the hotel room frantically trying to get dressed. Truth? We overslept! We were only going to be on national TV and we decide to sleep in!! OMG!!! Why is this happening???!!

Of course it didn't take the boys long to get dressed but Morgan and I were a different story. Levi was straightening my hair as I put on makeup. Lucas assisted Morgan, as she was stumbling around due to her cast.

And then all of a sudden the phone rang. I said "everyone be quiet!" I picked up the phone and a gentleman said "Ms Lyngaas?" I said, "Yes." very calmly. "Your chauffeur awaits". I responded with in a very calm and collective voice, "Great, thank you so much." I then hung up the phone and said, *"AHHHH !!! You got to be kidding me!" It is 7 o'clock !!! I shouted "OK you guys we got to go!! We got to go!!!" Levi said "yeah, we got to go.. We know."* Of course they know, they are teenagers. Silly me! On the other hand, *"if Mom is going to freak out, so are the kids. Right?"* We grabbed our coats and shoes and put them on in the elevator. Of course the boys were ready prior to this.

Jessica Lyngaas

As we appeared in the lobby, we all presented ourselves as very calm and collected and then boarded our limo for the ride to the studio. Rebecca our host from LifeSource said "you guys all look great! Did you sleep okay?" I smirked and said "Oh yes....We all just woke up 15 minutes ago!" She replied with "Wow, you all did good. I would have never known." Once we left the hotel my heart finally went back down into my chest as the 'rush' was over for a while.

Looking back at this day now, I know the Good Lord was watching over us and he wanted us to be well rested and did not want us to have any extra time on our hands to fret or anticipate what the day was going to bring us. Seriously, "Always be careful what you wish for." God has more power then us.

"To whom God was pleased to make known how great for the Gentiles are the riches of the glory of this mystery which is Christ within and among you. The hope of realizing the Glory." (Colossians 1:27)

"For you are may hope; O Lord God, You are my trust from my youth and the source of my confidence." (Psalm 71:5)

CHAPTER 11

Trust

It's hard to trust. This you must do with your heart. There are so many unknowns and it can be scary, but when you allow God to take the lead he is an avid guide...oh and by the way he's on duty 24 seven, 365 days a year, and is free of charge. All you have to do is love and obey. Dang!!!!

{We arrived at the Rockefeller Center plaza where the TODAY show is produced. As we got out of the Escalade immediately the paparazzi were there snapping pictures, left and right. Our chauffeur quickly escorted us inside the doors and we were greeted by a hostess who checked us in and then took us down to the area where they did our hair and make-up. After they had us ready to go they kept moving us around the 'set' as they did not want us to prematurely meet the recipient of Lance's organs. That was to happen on live TV!!!

As we came up the escalator which was next to the street window where the people stand outside to watch TODAY the people were screaming. My boys looked at me and said, "what is their problem?" and I told them they didn't know who we were and probably thought we were celebrities. The response I got from the kids was, "Obviously they do not know who we are or they would not be screaming."

In my heart and soul I felt they did know who we were and they were cheering us on. After all there is always Preview of the actual show. Even through the excitement and nervousness I felt, I kind of giggled, but at the same time was relieved that the kids were calm and cool about what would be occurring momentarily.

As we approached the set, they placed microphones on us and suddenly we heard, "Jessica, Levi, Lucas, and Morgan, please come out and meet the recipient of your Dad's heart, liver, and kidney.

I walked out first and Kirk got up and asked if he could have a hug and I told him, "Absolutely!" As he hugged me he kind of lifted me up just like Lance used to do. I then hugged Rita and it was the coolest thing. I stood back and observed my kids reactions as they hugged Kirk and Rita and then we all sat down...not even realizing we are on national TV.

The lights were so bright it was distracting enough to not look towards the cameras. I constantly had my priority on the kids and that keeping them calm and focused was my goal for the day. Ann Curry asked us "How do you feel knowing your Husband/Dad is still helping others?" All of a sudden my oldest son made the comment "I think it's pretty cool how my dad still lives on!"

I was amazed that any of them said anything and for a child to comprehend this extraordinary situation is beyond words. This was our first physical acquaintance with Kirk and Rita and a memorable indeed. Everyone was very complementary of the organ donation and compassionate with their genuine and kind words.

I then thought to myself trying to stay focused and listen to Ann Curry ask questions, I thought I am on TV right now. This gentleman has Lance's heart. Wow! I am humbled. It felt so good to hug Kirk. There was no doubt it felt like a warm, big hug from Lance.

After we were on TV we went down to the bottom floor of the Rockefeller center plaza and had a wonderful breakfast and visited with Kirk and Rita. This day is beyond words. While eating, visiting, and getting to know each other, I definitely starting looking at life as a precious precious Gift. An extraordinary milestone in our lives had occurred. An opportunity that occurred due to our Sovereign Lord. Oh, he is Divine!

People have asked me how I kept it together when I met Kirk and Rita, and through the whole interview? I really don't have an answer to this day, but what my heart tells me is that God was right there next to me, guiding me and my children and because I trust him to lead me to prosperous pastures and still waters, he kept me upright and functioning.

"Yes, though I walk through the valley of the shadow of death, I will fear or dread no evil, for You are with me; Your rod and Your staff they comfort me." (Psalm 23:4)

"Trust in the Lord with all your heart, and lean not unto your own understanding."
(Proverbs 3:5-6)

Jessica Lyngaas

CHAPTER 12

Gift

{After we ate breakfast we then started touring around the beautiful city of New York. We went to Central Park and took some neat pictures with each other as we played on the swings and then we went to the Christopher Columbus mall. While at the mall the six of us were coming down the escalator and as a woman was going up the escalator, she yelled at Kirk, "Hey! Weren't you just on the TODAY show this morning? Didn't you just receive organs from these kid's dad?"

She then ran up the escalator and got on the escalators coming down and visited with us at the bottom. She told us that morning she had 17 adults in her kitchen and now 12 became donors. They all went down to the DMV and switched on their driver's license to 'Donor'.

This particular encounter at the mall eight hours after we were on the Today Show was unbelievable. We are in a city of 8 million people and we are recognized 8 hours later? Twelve New Yorkers became donors that very day from one household? Unbelievable !!!

We are each God's gifts and we have been given gifts. The phrase that we hear often due to Lance being a donor is, "You have given the gift of life". It's not easy to comprehend and for that matter it's very mind-boggling and the neatest thing is each of us is a special gift that God created with his very own hands. Because God is so majestic, we as humans are able to continue to give the gift of life.

If that is not awesome, I don't know what is. Because God has a plan for each and every one of us we become gifted. I say that because God takes that 'difficult piece' of life out of the equation in our journey if we love, trust, and obey him. That difficult piece usually ends up being us as a human being attempting to be in control of the unknown, and trying to manage something that is not capable of being managed by our superficial, earthly, society-driven way.

I am not trying to say that if you have God in your life that you will not be up against difficult situations, but what I am saying is if we trust God, He will lead us in the right path. We may be on an unknown road and feel uneasy but if we trust and obey he will keep us safe.

The miracle of life is so incredible. For all of those who have been given the gift of a child, either living or deceased, it is easy to comprehend what I'm saying. The same can be said for those who are able to take part in continuing another life as a donor. Being part of a Donor Family continues to humble me and quiet my brain as I see the living results of Lance's organs giving life to others.

There was also others that benefited from Lance's organs. A middle-aged woman received Lance's other kidney and she stated "I no longer have to be on dialysis. Thank you so much for the gift of life. I now can be non dependent on a machine and I am able to enjoy my grandchildren."

Lance's femur bone was given to a child who was born with out a leg bone; his ulna bone given to a baby born with no arm; a skin graft for a burn victim was performed; and his corneas given to one who no longer had sight, and a few more donations. This awakening of how breathtaking donating life is continues to astonish me. Its miraculous and leaves me speechless.

When one chooses to be a donor and you are part of the family donating please understand that meeting the recipient is 100% an option. It will only take place if it is a mutual agreement from both the donor family and the recipient.

The impact of being part of a donor family and allowing my husband to help One to continue here on earth has given me a new prospective in life. It has not ever been easy for me to say

Oh _____(whatever the event may be) has changed my life! This my friend definitely has!! When I stop and evaluate the complex family I now have, I giggle with amazement. I thank the Lord for my life I have been given. I have had many trials, pain, and suffering and continue to have, but as I look around at my friends, family, community, and world; I would never wish for someone else' life. I have grown to be much more opened-minded, accepting, quiet, and content. This in return has given me more peace, joy, and love to share with others.

As I dry my tears and redo my make-up most days, I continue to be humbled with the many opportunities I am given. Writing this book is one of them.

For those who do not know how to become a donor I encourage you to go to the following websites listed on the Resource page of this book and learn the information and process that takes place. Another way to become a donor is to check the box on your drivers license that states, I wish to be an organ donor. If you are unsure if this is something you want to do, I encourage you to pray about it and ask God for his guidance and peace. It truly is an awesome experience and continues to be.

"Yes the Lord will give what is good, and our land will yield its increase. Righteousness shall go before him and shall make his footsteps a way in which to walk." (Psalm 85: 12-13)

Jessica Lyngaas

CHAPTER 13

Knowledge

{Returning home that very next morning at 12AM in Fargo, ND, the boys were anxious to start hunting in 7 hours. We were greeted by our wonderful neighbors and the hunting plan discussion began. I had much relief that we arrived back safely from New York and now our normal routine was back on track.

The hunting weekend was a huge success and the 12 hunters even shard their abundance of trophies with Lance. They all went down to the cemetery to show off their deer. Truth, Lance was with them all day long.}

As you begin your every morning do you go about your day and hide your talents, hording your valuable abilities, or do you share your smile and gifts with others? Can you share the love, peace, and joy that God has placed in your heart?

It is real easy to say "well of course I do or absolutely I can." Truth is, the answer is 'no' for many people, including myself. When tragedy hits and turmoil is raging, immediately falling into an 'idle mode' and having the last thing on your mind being 'sharing or giving'. Loving others, spreading joy and laughter, and living peacefully becomes distinct. This occurring as our mind and body have been traumatized and then we forget to seek our Redeemer for help.

We are all children of God therefore if you are reading this right now you are his child. He tells us to love others as we love ourselves. This isn't new information for most but because some may have forgotten this I promise you if you fall off the Lord's path of living, you can come back. Just ask God for forgiveness if need be and he will accept. He waits for our longing for him.

This piece of knowledge is very critical for all. Especially for one who is grieving a loss.

Think of this... If everything was simple and we did what we pleased and had no one to answer to including: rules, regulations, or others, why would we need anyone in our lives, especially God? We wouldn't. We are human beings We will make mistakes and we do not know everything we need to know.

Because we live in a complex world that has many different avenues to take, we need His constant hand of guidance. Through trial and error, experience and triumph, our definition of who we are will define what we will become.

Imagine this with me if you would. "Life Happens." What does that mean? It means major events, issues, and circumstance are going to occur and are you ready for them? I wasn't, and with the help of the good Lord, I danced my way through and still continue to.

Only gently expressing my experience, not promoting fear, but in the last 13 years I have experienced many 'unplanned parties'. The guest were coming to be entertained whether I had invited them or not. What kind of a hostess was I to be? Well personally I love being happy, giving, smile, and be full of joy. Unfortunately, 'Life' doesn't always allow this or doesn't allow these tasks to be simply done.

It all starts with having a good, logical, and positive attitude. A mistake that can be made is when we decide we know it all and no longer need to be taught. This is an awakening for me only because *"I've been here done this."*

When we have this attitude we are basically saying, "I've learned enough. I can do this I don't need anything else." Well, wakey wakey, you need something every day. Words of advice to everyone: never stop learning. With our frequently changing world, choosing not to learn new knowledge, you could end up living very miserable. Becoming stuck in a routine can create rigidity, a closed mind, and a wiliness of not compromising.

I get it. Change is not easy and can be scary. Realize too that just because you change up your routine or way of handling situations doesn't mean that your first way was wrong and this new way is right. We all do things primarily out of habit and that's okay.

Some can get a bit on the defensive side when routines are switched or done in a more productive manner, hence working smarter so one doesn't have to work harder. With the changing culture we are in, having a more open heart and mind feels more free and with less effort. We all learn from each other and it doesn't matter if your younger or older. Really focus and know that God created all of us. People, places, and time are placed in our path for a reason.

I made my mind up long ago that anytime I was given an opportunity to learn something new I would take it! I love and enjoy with all my heart learning new ideas, history, techniques, and wisdom, especially from those who have not or do not have an easy walk in life. Their focus seems so deep, genuine, and sincere. They've gone through their journey with a different outlook. When listening to them with an open mind, the ability of recognizing different, but positive perceptions will occur.

My grandfather James L Putnam who died 12/31/2014 at the age of 92 stated to me "You know Jessica, I'm so sorry you have had to go through what you have gone through at your small age. Just think, I never had to go through any of it and will never have too." I said "Papa, really? You have lived through the dirty thirties, the depression, etc...like that that was nothing to live through? "He said "We really have a society that portrays false beliefs. What virtues has God lay-ed out for us?" I looked at Papa for a while and was speechless (which usually I am not). Thinking deep I said "Alright.... I get it..."

We tend to put our focus in different areas from which those God wants us to put them in. We naturally can maintain and keep going with what we know or what we have done in the past, but seriously this eventually becomes tiring and unproductive.

Never stop learning. We have no idea of what God has in store for us. Instead of walking through life *in a tunnel*... seek God and wait for his direction. Choosing a life that is unwilling to learn new, may lead us to a life in which we will never know our full potential.

Besides gathering new knowledge, if you ever have an opportunity to teach something, please do so. Remember you were given a gift by a man who gave of himself so unselfishly don't be isolated-share.

"The Lord said to Moses, Behold, I will rain bread from the heavens for you, and the people shall go out and gather a day's portion everyday, that I may prove them whether they will walk in my law or not." (Exodus 16:4)

"For who has known or understood the mind of the Lord so as to guide and instruct him and give him knowledge? But we have the mind of Christ and do hold the thoughts of his heart." (I Coritnthians 2:16)

CHAPTER 14

Experience

Look back at all the things that you have experienced? Many things are thrown at us either because of the path we have chosen and wanted to experience, or sometimes just by chance as we walk through our journey in life.

Taking the time to listen when somebody begins to share an occurrence, event, or a very important time in their life with you, try to absorb all of it and give that person full attention with all your heart. Not only will you probably learn something new, but you may end up helping that person continue their walk in life.

The neatest thing I've enjoyed about working with my elders is the fact that they have experienced way more than I have and if given the opportunity, I will get a chance to inherit some new knowledge.

Being part of an extraordinary event, in our case a donor family, is hard to even fathom. But overall the number one thing I do understand is the fact that when one's time is up here on earth another's time perhaps has just begun. This entire process has had so much purpose and value that it comforts me to know that the motive Lance stood for continues to live in others. Taking life experiences, God's gifts, and sharing them with others can be a blessing that truly does make a difference!

In 2014 I had my first child's graduation from high school. The planning process was a bit daunting, but became very exciting and calming when I was informed that Kirk and Rita Watson were going to be visiting and we were ecstatic in anticipation of this huge milestone for both Levi and myself.

All our family and friends were able to meet these wonderful people and Kirk and Rita attended the graduation ceremony and celebration at our farm. Amazement filled my soul.

The most virtuoso moment during their visit happened just before they were going to leave for Colorado. Kirk told me he brought the video of the heart transplant that Mayo Hospital gave to him and asked me if I wanted to watch it. Naturally I enthusiastically agreed.

As the video began you can only imagine the fear of the unknown that consumed my brain. But within a minute the memories of what I saw, knew, and loved intrigued me and I was mesmerized.

{The week of Lance's death was very stormy and the details unforgettable as each storm left us with more yard to clean. The video began with the jet leaving Fargo in the pouring rain and landing in Rochester, MN. The team of Doctors walked off the plane and the organs, which were in a cooler, were taken to the operating room where Kirk was awaiting Lances' heart, liver, and kidney.}

Kirk was fully-prepped for transplant surgery and when Lance's heart arrived it was placed in a stainless steel basin filled with ice. Seeing Lance's heart was an awe-inspiring moment I had ever experienced.

You see, this heart was like a pearl. It was so pure, bright, and had an appearance of beauty and strength. The beauty and strength of Lance! There were many monitors and one of the telemetry monitors showed Kirk's vitals as they had him on life support.

A second telemetry monitor showed Kirk's vital signs after the transplant would be done and successful. So as we watched the video this 2nd monitor was blank and it showed asystole," as a straight line-absolutely no rhythm [a state of no cardiac electrical activity, hence no contractions of the myocardium and no cardiac output or blood flow. Asystole is one of the conditions required for a medical practitioner to certify death]"[1] As the surgeons and nurses diligently and precisely did their heroic job, their result was truly touched by God's hands and the telemetry monitor now showed a beautiful heart rate.

Yes, that is right! Lance's heart was beating, and beating strong, in Kirk! It was a perfect match!!! Truly, our God works miracles and they are astonishing. I was speechless. With tears of sadness and also much Joy.

Kirk was sitting right next to me on the couch. I just couldn't believe everything that had occurred. Honestly their isn't a day that goes by where I just shake my head and say to God "Wow, what you are and how you are so capable of doing.... Enormous things!"

That evening when I laid in bed I was filled with awe and delight that I had taken the time to watch the video. It has helped me to realize that though we cannot always see how God works in our lives, this miracle serves as a huge reminder that he is working and working like no human could ever imagine, and that we are not alone. He is always with us!!

"And Jesus, replying, said to them, Have Faith in God. Truly I tell you, whoever says to this mountain, be lifted up and thrown in the seal and does not doubt at all in his heart but believes that what he says will take place, it will be done for him. For this reason I am telling you, whatever you ask for in prayer, believe that it is granted to you, and you will." (Mark 11:22-24)

CHAPTER 15

Reality

What is real and what is not. This being so routine, but yet harsh and matter-of-fact to simple to believe. You may have heard or said, Welcome to reality!" usually in a context of sarcasm or to be negatively understood. What if it were presented in a positive manner? I believe it would be easier to accept.

Who made reality? I think we can all figure that out. Maybe if common courtesy, loving others, becoming parallel with our neighbor so alignment is present and One is not above or below. These could be some parts of reality that could be brought back into the reality of Life. Then faith may become more strong and natural in our society.

Here is reality in my world. I have become a widow, had several physical disabilities that do not plan on going away and now have resulted my situation with a loss of a job (outside of my home). I do not dwell in this soupy swamp. I think of it as an ocean and I keep swimming. How do I do it? I call up to my expert Guide and Founder. He keeps me going and moving forward. The more you practice the better you become at it. Always practice your Faith and the results are and will be rewarding!!

As stated earlier we live in this world where people are constantly compared to others. "Society knows best" because this is the 'Norm'.

Let's think about how it really should be. God created each and every one of us individually and because we are all 'wired' as individuals, comparing ourselves to others becomes a negative and false reality.

Unfortunately with all the amazing things in life like, technology which has created numerous items for all to enjoy; beautiful homes, comfortable vehicles, and computers-the list goes on and on.

The reality is we can't seem to live without more things, and we compare ourselves to how many "things" we have, compared to others. It can consume us so much that the small and simple things in life are missed.

I get it. Life is not always warm and fuzzy and, as a matter fact can be pretty cold and thorny, often determined by the mindset you want to accept and use as you travel this journey on earth!

What is the obvious reality for me right now? I am a widow raising two young handsome men and a beautiful young lady. I am the sole provider for our household and I am capable and will defeat all negative thoughts, doubt, jabs from others, and anything else destructive that tries to get into my life and destroy what God has created for me.

How do I do this? I can't do it alone therefore I walk daily with God as my savior, and I put all my burdens in his hands and then wait patiently for guidance. GOD IS SO GOOD. HE IS REAL, AND HE IS ALWAYS PRESENT. THIS IS REALITY!!!!! We may not see him in human form but he is constantly present in our everyday walk. Open your heart and mind to him. He is there waiting.

"He who believes in me as the scripture has said, from his innermost being shall flow springs and rivers of living water." (John 7: 38)

Look carefully then how you walk! Live purposefully and worthily and accurately, not as the unwise and witless, but as wise, making the very most of the time, because the days are evil. Therefore do not be vague and thoughtless and foolish, but under*standing and firmly grasping what the will of the Lord is."* *(Ephesians 5: 15-17)*

CHAPTER 16

Peace

When we turn on the TV or listen to the radio we hear about all the corruption in the world and we continually here we need to pray for peace. There's no doubt the Devil is diligently working to destroy, promote hate, and trying to disrupt our simple way of life.

When I was encouraged to write this book about our story I was asked "Jessica, do you know the message you want to get across to people? It is very powerful and I do not think you are even aware what you have to offer others." I thought about this for a while and it wasn't until about a year ago when my message fluently spoke to me.

Understand that No matter what the circumstance in life, whether Good, Bad, or Ugly, realize that with the help of God you will be able to survive, maintain your Faith and confidence, respect yourself, and most importantly love yourself and others.

When we are able to love and respect ourselves we will be able to love and respect others....thus creating true peace. While this may sound too simple, it is! It really is!!!

We as humans tend to amplify most things and then involve them to be much more complex than they need to be. We really do need to just 'keep it simple'. To keep it real and love. To love those who have hurt us the most. When we accept who we are and what God has created, the astonishment of what our blessings are, becomes so enormous that it can flood us with true peace, joy, and happiness.

We must guard our heart against vulnerability and bitterness. God has given us all the ability and strength to love. I encourage all to take the time to acknowledge that there is a God. If you chose to do so, peace will flow through you and through others as you become an example of what The Lord wants for all of us.

Know that if God is our Savor he will lead us to greener pastures. We just need to go to him and he will guide us and our inheritance of eternity in heaven is far more than anything we will ever see here on earth.

As the incredible journey continues, God has placed many seeds in my life to grow and nurture. He also put a very special person on my journey: Christopher Clark, my fiance. As Chris is my friend, lover, and companion, he encourages with enthusiasm, positivism, respect, and through his continual, supportive, unconditional love. He is true to his word, is a great listener, and is dedicated to our mutual purpose in life: to live each day according to God's word!

Just as Chris has observed so many setbacks through the last five years of my journey, and supported me through it all, he also has been able to see first-hand all the wonderful, amazing, and exciting ways our awesome God has enriched our lives! In times of trial when I am tempted to throw up my hands and just quit because my energy level has been depleted he will be the first one to simply respond respectively and encourage me lovingly.

Recently he said to me "How do you rebound so quickly and positively? You constantly have different issues or areas in your life that are so discouraging. How do you actually avoid the discouragement and just let them pass?"

My answer: Faith. Chris also reminded me I avoid discouragement by not letting it take and overwhelm me, and instead, embracing it and giving it to God. I really thought seriously about that exchange and realized I finally understood things will not happen without the power of our Lord.

Personally, it is exhausting for me to even begin to conquer the difficult and challenging, all alone. Lord knows, we will all have many obstacles, disappointments, and devastating losses in our lives. These will continue to as long as we are living here on Earth. Praise God for His eternal presence and support!

Chris and I have shared and will share many laughs, tears, frustrations, and joy but every day brings beams of love, support, and respect. I am confident to say, with God as our leader and our solid foundation, we are both very excited to start a new chapter in our life together and enjoy our six children as we grow old. I ask for your prayers for our united new family. Our special day is set for July 8, 2017.

Being quite aware that our society will continually flood this world with complexity, I will never lose interest and maintain my determination to seek and strive for simplicity. I want to leave you with this:

May the love of God touch each and every one of your hearts and I pray for peace and hope for all. God bless you all!! Amen. {enough said}

"For now the plans I have for you, declares the Lord, Plans to prosper you and not to harm you, plans to give you hope and a future." (Jeremiah 29:11)

The Lord your God is with you. He is mighty to save. He will take great delight in you he will quiet you with his love. He will rejoice over you with singing." (Zephaniah 3:17)

EPILOGUE

The Title of the book as **My Pulse** meaning this is my 'beat' in life; "Consistent and steady. Never wanting to skip a beat."[1] **His Will**, under the will of God, He is in control. Though there was much **Tragedy, Triumph** still stands. **Echoed her Faith;** With continuous guidance from up above the repetition of my faith prevails as I look at the journey that's been taken. I walk each day in faith with our ever so Awesome God! With him all things are possible

The 16 chapters of this book represent the 16 years Lance and I were married. Our 16th anniversary was celebrated assisting Lance to the Pearly Gates of Heaven.

My purpose in writing this book is to help others understand the importance of loving yourself and others after a horrible tragedy, and recognizing, through faith, that God will always be at your side. I wish you strength to stay confident with your inner self, finding comfort within from God and those around you, as you continue on your journey. Knowing that the life that left you is a gift from God to be treasured for your lifetime.

We are living in some difficult times that are going to be trying, but with God as our Savior we will not have to fight the battle on our own. All we really need to do is ask.

"Come to me, all you that are weary and are carrying heavy burdens, and I will give you rest." (Matthew 11:28)

RESOURCES

life.source.org (LifeSource organ and Tissue Donation covers Minnesota, North Dakota, and South Dakota)

donatelife.net (Donate Life America)

unos.org (United Network for organ sharing [UNOS])

restoresight.org (Eye Bank Association of America [EBAA])

The people who are employed by the above listed organizations are well trained, professional, and gifted individuals. Most people would realize not just anyone could do this type of career. Personally I want to say "thank you" to LifeSource as I feel you all have done a wonderful job for my children and I.

NOTES

Chapter 2: Finding and Maintaining Strength
1. Merriam-webster.com

Chapter 3: Purpose and Value
1. Merriam-webster.com

Chapter 4: Control
1. Jungwirth, Amy, "The Lance I Knew." 2011.

Chapter 5: Choices
1. Auber, Harriet, "Our blest Redeemer, ere. He breathed." Spirit of the Psalms by Harriet Auber, 1829.

Chapter 14: Experience
1. Merriam-webster.com

Epilogue
1. Merriam-webster.com

ACKNOWLEDGMENT

I want to thank my friends, family, and my coworkers for the extending of your helping hands, listening ears, bright smiles, and open hearts. Each has been a very important part of my journey thus far and serve as a continual reminder of how God places people in and out of our lives to show the example of what Love really is.

I Especially want to recognize Our Almighty Lord Jesus Christ for his continual and ongoing support; Lance Lyngaas for teaching me so much about life and being strong and always supportive to others; Christopher Clark your constant encouraging and listening ear, will never go unnoticed; Levi, Lucas, and Morgan Lyngaas where do I begin? You three have been my rock and without you I would not be where I am today. Though you have been right along side of me through all the hurdles, one would never know what has gone on and goes on in our 'little world.' You all are strong, respectful, hardworking, and kind individuals. Your a true reminder of what our purpose is here on earth and I am so very proud of all of you.

Kirk and Rita Watson, you have been an amazing gift to our family. Jacinta Putnam, Tessa Stroehl, Jerry and Deb Barnum, Julianna Paulsen, and Sandy Peckinpah I appreciate and thank you from the bottom of my heart for all your motivation, encouragement, knowledge you've shared, smiles, hugs, and laughter. The gift you all have is very inspiring.

I also want to acknowledge my grandparents, the Late James L Putnam and his wife, Betty. Your love, support, encouragement, and compassion have empowered me. Your continuous involvement through my life as a child, adolescent and then adult was ever so much appreciated! You always were an amazing example to follow and I love and miss you very much!